Introduction to Medjugorje

Introduction to Medjugorje

Mark Miravalle

QUEENSHIP PUBLISHING

DECLARATION

The declaration of the Congregation for the Propigation of the Faith, A.A.S. 58, 1186 (approved by Pope Paul VI on October 14, 1966) states that the **Nihil Obsta**t and **Imprimatu**r are no longer required on publications that deal with private revelations, provided they contain nothing contrary to faith and morals.

The author wishes to manifest his unconditional submission to the final and official judgement of the Magisterium of the Church regarding the events presently under investigation at Medjugorje.

Library of Congress Number: 2004111864

Published by:
    Queenship Publishing
    P.O. Box 220
    Goleta, CA 93116
    (800) 647-9882 (805) 692-0043 FAX: (805) 967-5843
    http://www.Queenship.org

Printed in the United States of America

ISBN: 1-57918-265-8

Contents

PREFACE TO THE SECOND EDITION

I am most grateful to Queenship Publishing for their kind invitation to re-publish this little work on Medjugorje, which first appeared several years ago under the title, *Heart of the Message of Medjugorje*. Although cited references from the Papal Magisterium come from the earlier years of Pope John Paul II's inspired pontificate, they nevertheless reflect the perennial teachings of our holy Catholic faith and remain quintessentially relevant to the serious needs and crises facing the Church and the world today, as do the celestial words of the Queen of Peace.

What is presently the official Church position concerning the Marian apparitions at Medjugorje? Our minds and hearts must always be in obedience to the final and definitive judgment provided by the Holy See and proper ecclesiastical authority in union with the Holy See.

On April 10, 1991, the Bishops' Conference of the former Yugoslavia issued a declaration entitled, "Declaration of the Ex-Yugoslavia Bishops' Conference on Medjugorje." While the declaration is inconclusive, stating that at this point of the investigation "it cannot be affirmed that one is dealing with supernatural apparitions and revelations," it then goes on to state that "the faithful journeying to Medjugorje, prompted both by motives of belief and other motives, require attention and pastoral care" by the Bishop of Mostar and his brother bishops while the investigation continues.

This declaration makes clear that the Medjugorje apparitions are at present *neither formally approved ("constat de supernaturalitate") nor formally condemned ("constat de non supernaturalitate")*, but represent a middle category of Church evaluation referred to as *"non constat de supernaturalitate,"* which allows for both continued personal belief in the apparitions and personal (non-diocesan sponsored) pilgrimages to Medjugorje while the investigation is ongoing.

The legitimacy of personal belief in the Medjugorje apparitions and personal pilgrimages to the apparition site at this time has been confirmed directly by the Holy See in a statement by the Congregation for the Doctrine of the Faith, issued on May 26, 1998 (Protocol Number 154/81–06419) and signed by former Secretary to Cardinal Ratzinger, Archbishop Tarcisio Bertone.

In his letter to French Bishop, Msgr. Gilbert Aubry, Archbishop Bertone confirms the 1991 Declaration of the former Yugoslav Bishops' Conference: "As for the credibility of the 'apparitions' in question, this Dicastery respects what was decided by the bishops of the former Yugoslavia in the Declaration of Zadar, April 10, 1991." Further, Archbishop Bertone establishes that the personal opinions of Bishop Peric, local bishop of Mostar, against the authenticity of the apparitions, an opinion in disagreement with the former Yugoslav Bishop's 1991 Statement, represent simply "what is and remains his personal opinion," and therefore does not represent the official position of the Holy See nor of the former Yugoslav Conference. The Congregation's statement ends by confirming the legitimacy of personal and private pilgrimages that do not infer official approval of the events while further examination takes place.

In sum, the Holy See and the local Church authority confirmed by the Holy See in the body of the former Yugoslavian Bishops Conference, permit personal belief in the authenticity of the Medjugorje apparitions and in non-diocesan pilgrimages to Medjugorje as the Church continues its investigation and evaluation. Such is the wisdom of Holy Mother Church in matters of Marian private revelation: open, but cautious; do not "stifle the Spirit" (1 Thess. 5:19), but always "test the Spirit"(1 Thess. 5:21).

On a personal note, the messages of the Queen of Peace have been the means for great personal grace and blessing, particularly in regards to our family's humble efforts towards family prayer and sanctification. I am grateful for the freedom and privilege which the Magisterium presently provides that allows me to voice my strongest possible personal belief in the authenticity of the apparitions and messages of the Queen of Peace in Medjugorje, and I pray for the guidance of the Holy Spirit through the Immaculate Heart of Mary for the

Church's ongoing evaluation and eventual declaration of supernatural authenticity.

Dr. Mark Miravalle
Professor of Theology and Mariology
Franciscan University of Steubenville
June 25, 2004

INTRODUCTION

On June 24, 1981, six Croatian youths reported an apparition of the Blessed Virgin Mary in the small Croatian mountain town of "Medjugorje" (pronounced Med-ju-gor-ee-ay). Today, over twenty-two years and approximately thirty million pilgrims later, the visionaries continue to report apparitions and messages from the "Gospa," as they refer to her. These messages are both a profound and urgent plea to the contemporary world regarding its present moral state and, consequently, its future.

This book makes no explicit statement regarding the supernatural character of the apparitions. This official judgement can be made only by the teaching authority of the Catholic Church (the Magisterium). The events in Medjugorje are presently under investigation and the author wishes to affirm his unconditional readiness to accept the final judgement of the Church.

The focus of this book is the "message" of Medjugorje. We will examine the actual contents of the messages reported by the young visionaries and attributed to the Blessed Virgin Mary. The other reported phenomena (solar miracles, miraculous healings, nature of apparitions, etc.) will be discussed only as they relate to the reported message, either directly of by way of the context. The purpose of this book is to present a summary of the message's core elements for the individual who has neither the time nor the desire for a thorough examination. For a more comprehensive treatment of the topic, especially as it is rooted in the various sources of revealed Christian truth, I refer you to *The Message of Medjugorje: The Marian Message to the Modern World*, originally published by University Press of America, Lanham, Maryland, 1985.

There are two "pastoral" counsels which will help orientate the reader to the material in this book. They were offered by the visionary Marija during our conversation in May 1985.

First, the message of the Madonna is not solely for the people of Medjugorje, nor for the surrounding region, but the messages are designated for the entire world. The Madonna has stated, "The world is my parish, but there are many hearts not open to my words."

Secondly, Marija stressed that the revealed messages of Our Lady must be kept **objective**. The directives of prayer and penance are not to be changed or reduced even though they may be challenging. Once a revealed message is altered by those spreading the message, it becomes that of the human conveyor, not of the heavenly messenger. Marija emphasized the need for each individual to incorporate gradually the ascetical directives of prayer and penance to the degree that is prudent for each individual. Marija referred to her own integration of the Medjugorjian message over a five-year period.

The Madonna's first request for prayer consisted of the Creed, seven Our Father's, Hail Mary's and Glory Be's. Marija didn't know how she could fit that much prayer into her day. She had the same response with the later Marian requests for the five-decade rosary, then the full fifteen-decade rosary, and finally the request for three hours of daily prayer. Marija turned to me and said, "But now, I want to pray always." There have been profound spiritual effects from Marija's gradual but persevering efforts to incorporate the Medjugorje message in her life.

The global nature of the message of Medjugorje and the need to remain objective but personal in the implementation of the spiritual directives of the Madonna convey two important guiding principles to help us "live the messages" day by day.

In order to understand and incorporate the message of Medjugorje we will examine the relevant background to the apparitions, point out basic themes in the messages and show how they complement both scripture and the post-conciliar teachings of Vatican II. Then we will examine Medjugorje in light of the approved Marian apparitions at the Lourdes and Fatima. The last chapters of the book contain the messages attributed to the Virgin Mary that have been translated into English and specific prayers revealed at Medjugorje.

Chapter I

Background

A brief word on the key events, locations, and individuals involved in the Medjugorje event will assist us in understanding the identity and authority of those transmitting the messages as well as the significance of the words attributed to the Virgin Mary.

On June 24, 1981, two young women, along with some friends, claimed to have seen a vision of a beautiful young woman standing on a hillside just beyond the small village of Bijakovici in the parish of Medjugorje. The vision lasted 45 minutes. The following day the young women felt drawn to return to the spot. From the bottom of the hill the girls could clearly see the Vision high up on the hill, Podbrdo. These were the beginnings of the apparitions at Medjugorje.

Medjugorje: The Parish, the People, the Apparitions

The parish of St. James in Medjugorje is located in a valley surrounded by low rambling mountains. Vineyards surround the parish land on three sides. The people live a poor and simple lifestyle in this agricultural area. Before the apparitions began the spiritual state of the parish was much like any other in this land, a country that was communist when the apparitions began. Since then there has been such a considerable renewal of the sacramental life and basic Christian living that pilgrims are strikingly aware of the prevailing atmosphere of friendliness and Christian charity.

The apparitions originally took place on the hillside. Within days the gathering of large crowds created tensions with local government authorities. The pastor, who was under pressure from the local authorities, moved the gathering of people to the church for rosary and Mass. In August 1981 the police cordoned off the area of the hill and people were forbidden to go there any longer. From that time on, the apparitions took place in various private homes until the beginning of 1982. Then, at the request of the pastor expressed through the visionaries, the Virgin agreed to meet with them in the church.

The location of the apparitions has changed several times since the original apparition site. The apparitions later took place in a small room off the sanctuary of the church, then in the rectory and still later in the balcony (choir loft) of the church. Adaptations continue to be made for the precise location of the apparitions. Before each apparition, the visionaries pray the rosary along with the congregation. Mass is celebrated and confessions are heard daily.

The Visionaries

At the time of the first apparitions the seers were from ten to sixteen years of age. From youngest to oldest, the names of the youths are: Jakov Colo (male, born June 3, 1971), Ivanka (Ivankovic) Elez (female, born April 21, 1966), Ivan Dragicevic (male, born May 25, 1965), Marija Pavlovic (female, born April 1, 1965), Mirjana Dragicevic (female, born March 18, 1965), and Vicka Ivankovic (female, born July 3, 1964).

The following is an assessment of the visionaries in the first few years of the apparitions. Vicka, the oldest of the visionaries, is considered to be the most outgoing of the seers and does most of the talking during the apparitions. She is strong-willed but pleasant, usually has a big smile on her face, and is the most willing of the visionaries to answer the numerous questions of visiting pilgrims. In the past, Vicka has had several serious medical conditions, including an inoperable brain cyst, but she sees her physical suffering as redemptive suffering, and offers her pain as a reparational sacrifice to God.

Mirjana has been called the most "educated" of the visionaries. She left Medjugorje to study at the University in Sarajevo, a city three hours from Medjugorje. Mirjana was the first to receive all ten "secrets," which constitute events that will have an effect on the entire world. Although Mirjana no longer sees daily apparitions of the Virgin Mary, she continues to play a vital role in the Medjugorjian event. Mirjana has reported the following message from Our Lady at her last daily apparition: "Now you have to turn to God through faith like everyone else. I will appear to you on your birthday and when you encounter difficulties in life." According to Mirjana, Our Lady has disclosed the dates on which the different secrets will come to pass. Three days before one of the admonitions, Mirjana will notify a priest of her choice who, in turn, may choose to do what he wants with the information.

Marija is considered to be the "contemplative" of the visionaries. She has a clear serenity and peace even in the midst of the sometimes imprudent demands upon her time. It is through Marija that the "Thursday Messages" to the parish were given. Marija's disposition towards prayer and contemplation seems to set her apart as the most spiritually mature of the seers.

Ivan, the oldest of the two male visionaries, is more withdrawn than the others and does not encourage questions from the crowds. In August of 1981 Ivan had entered the seminary, but found the studies too difficult at that time because of his previous educational preparation. In June 1987, he completed his obligatory military duty for the state and returned to Medjugorje. While in the military he received apparitions only when off duty and at the home of a friend. Ivan, like Marija, seems to have a greater inclination to interior prayer and likewise possesses a more quiet disposition.

Ivanka has been called the "pretty visionary." From early on she did not see herself entering religious life, and in December 1986, married a young man from Medjugorje. In May 1985, Ivanka received the tenth secret from the Madonna and her daily apparitions ceased. However, the Madonna promised Ivanka an apparition annually on June 25, the anniversary date of the Medjugorjian apparitions, for the rest of her life.

Finally, there's Jakov, the youngest of the visionaries, who at the beginning of the apparitions had found it challenging to make it through the three-hour evening Mass services at Medjugorje. Although he was young when the apparitions first began, he had an exceptional ability to outwit the less than admirable efforts by visiting clergy and pilgrims to discover the contents of the secrets.

Jelena Vasilj (female, born May 14, 1972) is frequently called the "seventh visionary." Since December 15, 1982, Jelena has experienced messages from the Blessed Virgin Mary by means of inner locutions, hearing Our Lady, in Jelena's words, "within her heart." The messages given to Jelena are usually spiritual counsels and guidance for the interior life and growth in holiness for the parish prayer group.

Along with Jelena, there is another woman, Mirjana Vasilj (no relation), who reported the same type of charism as Jelena, but at the time the nature of her dialogue with Our Lady seemed to be primarily that of personal spiritual direction.

Twenty-fours years later, the six, known as the "visionaries," now range in age from thirty-three to forty years of age. Vicka lives with her husband Mario in the village of Gruda, just north of Medjugorje and they expect their second child in October of 2004. Mirjana is living in Medjugorje and has two daughters with her husband Marko. Marija, currently living in Italy, is married, and has four children. She visits Medjugorje a number of times each year. Ivan is also married and resides half the year in the parish of Medjugorje, and half the year in Boston, Massachusetts with his wife and their three children. Ivanka lives in Medjugorje, with her husband, has three children, with a fourth due in August 2004. Jakov is also still in Medjugorje and has a wife and three children of his own. The two locutionists, Jelena and Mirjana Vasilj, have also married and live in Medjugorje with their families.

The Types of Messages

The overall messages reported by the visionaries fall into four basic divisions: Personal Dialogue, Secrets, Information for Later Disclosure, and Principal Messages.

The messages given in Personal Dialogue consist of discussions concerning the daily life of the visionaries, assistance in their individual spiritual lives, and, sometimes, pilgrims' personal questions or petitions. The intimate nature of these messages and their personal focus makes them irrelevant to the general discussion of the message of Medjugorje. However, a few personal messages have been included because of their bearing on the general content of the messages.

The "Secrets" consist of ten messages that Our Lady has promised to confide to the visionaries that, for the most part, effect the entire world.

All six visionaries state that the secrets have a global significance. Part of one of the ten secrets has been disclosed by the youths. It consists of a sign promised by Our Lady that is to appear at the site of the first apparition. Our Lady has given a few specific messages about this sign. "This sign will be given for the unbelievers. You faithful already have signs, and you yourselves must become the signs for the unbelievers." According to the visionaries, many healings and miracles will follow the sign; but for those who believe, the time that precedes the sign is not a time for waiting, but a time for deeper conversion and special graces. "You faithful must not wait for the sign before you convert. Convert soon, for this time is a time of grace for you. This time is for deepening your faith and your conversion. When the sign comes, it will be too late for many."

Our Lady has also given information to the visionaries that will be disclosed at a later time. For example, Vicka reports that Our Lady has told her aspects of her life on earth, while Ivanka has been informed about future world events which are to be disclosed to the church authorities at the time designated by the Madonna.

The fourth division of the messages, the Principal Messages, will be our main focus. The Principal Messages are those words of Our Lady that are relevant not only to all Christians but to anyone who has, in the words of Our Lady, "an open heart." These messages are conveyed through the six visionaries, either collectively or as individuals, as the result of Mary's appearances and communication with them. The second source of principal messages is Jelena Vasilj, the "seventh visionary." As previously explained, Jelena has the gift of inner locutions.

This brief background provides the context in which the message of Medjugorje can be studied and understood. The seers of Medjugorje follow the pattern Our Lady often uses in designating whom she chooses to become transmitters of heavenly messages: children of simple and humble origins, who fail to have the level of education that could lead to the contamination of the heavenly message which the Mother of All Peoples wishes to bestow upon all of humanity through them.

Chapter II

Heart of the Message of Medjugorje

Peace through faith, prayer, fasting, penance, and conversions summarize the heart of the Madonna's messages according to the visionaries. These six foundational themes are the basis of the message of Medjugorje upon which other important elements, such as the rosary and daily Mass are developed. In the following two chapters these themes and their conformity to Church teaching will be discussed.

We will take up each theme by examining individual messages given by the visionaries and then look at how that same theme appears in the Gospels. The similarity between the message of Medjugorje as it appears in these themes and the identical themes found in the Gospels affirms the sound Christian doctrine contained in the reported Marian message.

"Believe Firmly"

The message of Medjugorje indicates both a general summons to a more committed faith in God and to a specific belief in the apparitions themselves.

The call to faith has been central and crucial to the message of Medjugorje since the beginning of the apparitions. On the sixth day of the reported appearances, Our Lady requested faith from everyone present.

> *Visionaries*: Dear Madonna: What do you wish from these people?
>
> *Our Lady*:   There is one God and one faith. Believe firmly.

The first spiritual directive specified by Our Lady was faith. According to an interview with Mirjana in 1983, "She (Our Lady) always recommended **faith**, prayer, and fasting." Our Lady has also spoken of the necessity of prayer to sustain a living faith, saying, "Faith cannot be alive without prayer."

There is also a specific call to have faith in the authenticity of the apparitions themselves. On June 26, 1981, the third day of the apparitions, the visionaries asked Our Lady for a specific message for priests. Our Lady responded, "Let the priests firmly believe." Vicka requested a miracle that would prove to others that Mary's appearances were authentic. Our Lady replied, "Let those who do not see believe as if they see."

Our Lady has also promised a visible sign on Podbrdo, the hill of the first apparition, for the "unbelievers," to help them believe in the apparitions. The time before the sign is to be one of profound graces, and she warned those with a living faith not to wait for the sign to begin the path to deeper faith and conversion.

> You faithful must not wait for the sign before you convert. Convert soon, for this time is a time of grace for you. You can never thank God enough for the grace God has given you. This time is for deepening your faith and your conversion. When the sign comes, it will be too late for many.

The Gospels emphasize a living faith also. As in Medjugorje, faith is the gateway both to the miraculous on earth and the glories and salvation of eternal life in heaven.

St. John speaks of the effects of faith in the following passages:

> For God so loved the world that He gave His only Son, that whoever believes in Him should not perish but have eternal life (Jn 3:16).
>
> For this is the will of My Father, that everyone who sees the Son and believes in Him should have eternal life; and I will raise him up on the last day (Jn 6:40).

Miracles can happen as the result of strong faith in God. We see this in the story of the woman with a hemorrhage (Mt 9:20-22). Her faith was initial to her healing, "Your faith has made you well." Faith is the key to the power of God at work among us as seen in this passage from St. Matthew:

> Jesus answered them, "Truly I say to you, if you have faith and never doubt, you will not only do what has been done to the fig tree, but even if you say to this mountain 'Be taken up and cast into the sea,' it will be done. And whatever you ask in prayer, you will receive, if you have faith" (Mt 21: 20-22).

The Gospel call for a living faith is every bit as crucial today as it was in the time of Christ. Jesus Christ still asks this question, "Nevertheless, when the Son of Man comes, will He find faith on earth" (Lk 18:8)?

The summons to faith is the same in the Gospels and in the message of Medjugorje: a committed faith in Christ which leads to the Father and to eternal salvation, and is the condition for the miraculous on earth.

Pray, Pray, Pray!

The Medjugorjian message emphatically calls for a greater generosity in prayer, both in quantity and intensity, as an indispensable means in attaining the peace of Christ in our hearts.

Several of the Thursday Messages have simply been a repeated exhortation for more prayer, as seen in the message on April 19, 1984: "Dear children, sympathize with me. Pray, pray, pray!" A later Thursday Message asked for a decrease in work and an increase in prayer: "These days you have been praying too little and working too much. Pray, therefore. In prayer you will find rest" (July 5, 1984).

Active prayer is a necessity in living the full message of Medjugorje:

> Dear children, I am calling you to an active approach to prayer. You wish to live everything I am telling you, but you do not get results from your efforts because you do not pray. Dear children, I beg you: open yourselves and begin to pray. Prayer will be joy. If you begin, it will not be boring because you will pray with pure joy (March 20, 1986).

Through Jelena, Our Lady specifically set the amount and degree of prayer for a youth prayer group in Medjugorje that began in June, 1983:

> Pray three hours a day...You pray too little. Pray at least half an hour in the

morning and evening; and further when I say, "Pray, pray, pray," I do not mean only to increase the hours of prayer but increase the desire to pray and to be in contact with God, to be in a continuous prayerful state of mind.

On June 4, 1983, Our Lady reportedly said:

You have begun to pray three hours, but you look at your watches, preoccupied with your work. Be preoccupied with the one thing necessary, and let yourself be guided by the Holy Spirit.

It is evident that the Medjugorjian message is calling for a greater generosity and quality of individual prayer than ever before.

The importance of prayer is clearly stated in the Gospels by Christ's own example:

...And in the morning, a great while before day, He rose and went out to a lonely place, and there He prayed (Mk 1:35).

And after He had dismissed the crowds, He went up into the hills by Himself to pray. When evening came He was still there alone (Mt 14:23).

And in the Gospel of John, Jesus prays for those who believe in Him:

> I am not praying for the world, but for those whom Thou hast given Me, for they are Yours, and I am glorified in them…I do not pray that Thou shouldst take them out of the world, but that Thou shouldst keep them from the evil one…I do not pray for these only, but also for those who believe in Me through their word, that they may all be one; even as Thou, Father, art in Me, and I in Thee…(Jn 17: 9–10, 10, 20–21).

Jesus illustrates the necessity of prayer, particularly in the midst of trial. He prepared Himself, by prayer on the Mount of Olives, for the Passion.

Jesus taught the disciples how to pray in the words of the "Our Father." This prayer summarizes how and for what Christians should pray (cf. Mt 6: 7–13; Lk 11:24).

The powerful effect of prayer is conclusively stated by our Lord: "Therefore I tell you, whatever you ask for in prayer, believe that you will receive it, and you will" (Mk 11:24–25).

The call to pray unceasingly, to pray in the midst of trial, to pray for conversions, to pray as a community, and to pray so as to disarm the efforts of Satan is found in the Gospels and is one of the essential themes of the Medjugorjian message.

Fasting From the Heart

One of the distinguishing marks of the message of Medjugorje is a call to return to the Christian practice of fasting. The neglect of this powerful spiritual discipline was the topic of the message on July 21, 1982: "Christians have forgotten they can prevent war and even natural calamities by prayer and fasting."

The Madonna complained about the virtual disappearance of fasting in the Church and initially asked the faithful to fast on Fridays. She said that almsgiving by the healthy is not a legitimate substitution for fasting. Those too ill to fast can choose some other form of sacrifice along with the reception of the Sacrament of Confession and Holy Communion.

Near the beginning of the apparitions, the visionaries asked Our Lady what was the best fast. She replied, "A fast of bread and water." During an unexpected appearance to Ivan on August 14, 1984, Our Lady requested a strict fast twice a week, on Wednesdays and Fridays.

However, fasting must be done with devotion and love in order to be effective. The Thursday Message, reported by Marija on September 20, 1984, concerns the quality of people's fasting:

Dear children, today I ask you to start fasting from the heart. There are many people who fast, but only because everyone else is fasting. It has become a custom which no one wants to stop. I ask the parish to fast out of gratitude to God for having let me remain this long in the parish. Dear children, fast and pray with your hearts.

The renewed practice of fasting is a principal means of living the message of Medjugorje:

I wish to tell you, dear children, to renew living the messages that I have given you. In particular, live the messages regarding fasting, because your fasting gives me joy. And so you will attain the fulfillment of all the plans God has for you here in Medjugorje (Sept. 26, 1985).

Fasting for the body and prayer for the soul constitute two of the strongest Medjugorjian calls for the spiritual well-being of the human person.

The Gospels often refer to the spiritual discipline of fasting. Again, Christ is the pre-eminent model of true fasting:

> Jesus was led by the Spirit into the wilderness to be tempted by the devil. And he fasted forty days and forty nights, and afterwards was hungry. And the temptor came and said to Him, "If you are the Son of God, summon these stones to become loaves of bread." But he answered, "It is written, 'man shall not live by bread alone, but every word that proceeds from the mouth of God'" (Mt 4:1-5).

Furthermore, Christ simply presumed His disciples would fast:

> And **when** you fast, do not look dismal, like the hypocrites, for they disfigure their faces that their fasting may be seen by men. Truly, I say to you, they have their reward. But when you fast, anoint your head and wash your face, that your fasting may not be seen by men buy by Your heavenly Father who is in secret; and Your Father who sees you in secret will reward you (Mt 6:6-18).

The disciples of John questioned Jesus why His disciples did not fast as did the Pharisees and themselves. Jesus replied that when the bridegroom departed, the disciples of Christ would also fast (Mt 9:14-16).

Our Lord attested to the profound power that comes from fasting when it is united with fervent prayer. The story of the possessed boy whom the disciples could not cure highlights the spiritual force of prayer and fasting against the presence of evil. The message of Medjugorje clearly parallels this Gospel principle:

> The disciples approached Jesus at that point and asked Him privately, "why could we not expel it?" "Because you have so little trust," He told them. "I assure you, if you had faith the size of a mustard seed, you would be able to say to this mountain, 'Move from here to there,' and it would move. This kind does not leave but by prayer and fasting" (Mt. 17: 19-21).

Fasting twice a week was a regular practice in the early church as well. A striking similarity with the message of Medjugorje is found in the Didache, authored between 60 and 120 A.D. by the early Christian community: "But do not let your fasts be with the hypocrites, for they fast on Mondays and Thursdays; but **you shall fast on Wednesday and Friday**" (Did 8:1).

Penance for the Salvation of Souls

Penance — a general call to deny oneself for the sake of Christ, the Church, and the spiritual growth of the individual — is a fundamental Medjugorjian theme. Apart from fasting, which is one specific form of penance, there is a general directive involving sacrifice and self-denial.

Penance has been continually stressed throughout the apparitions in Medjugorje. Shortly after the beginning of the apparitions, Our Lady asked the visionaries to climb to the top of the Mountain of the Cross at approximately two o'clock in the morning to pray that people would do penance for the conversion of sinners. An example of the importance of this theme is seen in the Thursday Message of July 26, 1984, "Dear children, today I would like to call you to persistent prayer and penance…"

In an interview in 1983, Marija was asked if Our Lady had given any specific messages for priests and bishops. She replied, "No, but a long time ago she said that they should accept us, help us as much as they can, and pray more and do penance…"

The report sent to Pope John Paul II by Father Tomislav Vlasic and the visionaries states that the ultimate goal of both penance and prayer is the salvation of souls: "The invitation to prayer and penance is meant to avert evil and war, but most of all to save souls."

The penitential call seems to be emphasized particularly during the Lenten season. Our Lady asked for great self-denial, as is seen in this Lenten message from 1986: "Dear children, this Lent is a special incentive for you to change. Start from this moment. Turn off the television and renounce other things which are useless."

The summons to penance is certainly present in the Gospels. Penance as a category can be all-encompassing. For example, the evangelical counsels, fasting, and the very crucifixion of Christ all constitute forms of penance. For our purpose, we will look at penance in the Gospels as all forms of self-denial undertaken for the sake of a person's spiritual growth.

In the Gospel of Matthew, denial of unruly desires and acts of physical mortification in order to safeguard spiritual life are established as a principle of the Christian life:

> If your right eye causes you sin, pluck it out and throw it away; it is better that you lose one of your members than that your whole body be thrown into hell. And if your right hand causes you to sin, cut it off and throw it away; it is better that you lose one of your members than that your whole body go into hell (Mt 5:27-30).

The cost of discipleship is total renunciation of self and acceptance of the "daily cross" in imitation of Christ as seen in Mark 8:34-36:

> If anyone wants to be a follower of Mine, let him renounce himself, take up his cross and follow Me. For anyone who wants to save his life will lose it, but

anyone who loses his life for the sake of
the Gospel will save it.

Penance is consistently stressed in the Gospels as
a powerful and effective means of conversion. This is
exemplified, but not exhausted, in the physical self-denial
of fasting. The emphasis on penance in the message of
Medjugorje is soundly established as a scriptural call.

Conversion of the Heart

The apparitions began on the feast of St. John
the Baptist, June 24. The universal call to conversion
for both believer and non-believer alike in the message
of Medjugorje strongly evokes St. John's gospel cry to
"Repent! The Kingdom of God is at hand" (Mt 1:2; Mk
1:4; Lk 3:3, 7-8).

Conversion for the believer means to turn
one's heart toward God and away from sin to an ever-
deepening degree, experiencing greater faith through
contrition. For the unbeliever, conversion is the call
to have faith in the one true God and to turn from sin
through repentance. Mary's urgent plea, in the spring of
1983, shows this dual nature of conversion:

> Hasten your conversion. Do not wait for
> the sign that has been announced for the
> unbelievers; it will already be too late
> for them to have a conversion. You who

believe, be converted, and deepen your faith.

Mirjana has spoken with the same sense of immediacy: "I say to all people, 'Convert' — the same as she did. 'Convert while there's still time.'"

The Medjugorjian message is not only personal and individual but universal in scope, as recorded in the message of April 1983:

> The only word I wish to speak is for the conversion of the whole world. I wish to speak it to the whole world. I ask nothing but conversion...It is my desire...Be converted...Leave everything; that comes from conversion.

There is a desperate need for prayer for the conversion of sinners throughout the world. On several occasions Our Lady has requested a greater increase of prayer and penance for this specific cause: "Pray these days for the conversion of sinners" (August 2, 1984), and further, "Let all the prayers which you say in your houses in the evenings be for the conversion of sinners, because the world is in great sin" (October 8, 1984).

The depth of suffering and sorrow the Madonna has for the world is beautifully expressed in the message given through Jelena:

> Where are your prayers? My gown which
> is usually radiant with light is now wet
> with tears. Oh, if you only knew how
> much the world sins; enter a little deeper
> into the world and you will see. It appears
> to you not to sin because you are in a
> peaceful world where there isn't disorder.
> But how many have tepid faith, and so do
> not listen to Jesus. If only you knew how
> much I suffer, you would not sin again.
> Oh, how I need your prayers. Pray!

The means for true conversion — greater faith, prayer, penance, fasting, and the Sacrament of Penance — have been stressed by Our Lady since the beginning of the apparitions, June 26, 1981:

> Men must be reconciled with God and
> with one another. For this to happen, it is
> necessary to believe, to pray, to fast, and
> to go to Confession.

Mary's directive for monthly sacramental Confession as a principal means of conversion will be further discussed in the following chapter.

Conversion to God and aversion from sin and self in synonomous with the Good News of salvation. Jesus appeared in Galilee proclaiming the good news of God: "This is the time of fulfillment. The reign of God is at hand! Reform your lives and believe in the gospel" (Mk 1:15).

John the Baptist "proclaimed a baptism of repentance which led to forgiveness of sins" (Lk 3:3). He demanded some external sign of interior conversion of heart of the crowds that flocked to hear him:

> You brood of vipers, who warned you to flee from the wrath to come? Bear fruit that befits repentance...Even now the axe is laid to the root of the tree. Every tree, therefore, that does not bear good fruit is cut down and thrown into the fire (Lk 3: 7-9).

Christ identifies His mission with the universal call to conversion in this passage from Luke 5:30-32:

> Those who are well have no need for a physician, but those who are sick; I have not come to call the righteous, but **sinners to repentance.**

Jesus describes the heavenly joy over the conversion of a single sinner in the parable of the lost sheep:

> Which one of you, having a hundred sheep, if he has lost one of them, does not

> leave the ninety-nine in the wilderness,
> and go after the one which is lost until
> he finds it? And when he has found it,
> he lays it on his shoulders, rejoicing...Just
> so I tell you, there will be more joy in
> heaven over one sinner who repents than
> over ninety-nine righteous persons who
> need no repentance" (Lk 15: 4-7).

Repentance is the essential scriptural element for true conversion. It brings about forgiveness of sins (Mk 1:4), and enables faith to grow to maturity (Mk 1:15). Consistent failure to repent or to turn continually from self to God will result in rejection by the Son of Man on the day of judgement (Mt 11:20-24; Lk 12:8-10). Jesus quickly eliminates the idea that those who die tragically are more in need of conversion than anyone else:

> Do you think that these Galileans were
> worse sinners than all the other Galileans,
> because they suffered thus? I tell you, no;
> but unless you repent you will likewise
> perish (Lk 13: 2-4).

The Medjugorjian theme of conversion stresses the same elements of repentance, faith, and the continual need to turn to God and away from sin as is found in the Gospels. Both emphasize the need to "hasten your conversion" or "likewise perish."

The Peace of Christ

The most important theme of the Medjugorjian message is that of peace. However, it is also the most easily misunderstood aspect of the message. The peace Our Lady calls for is the peace of Christ in the soul and not primarily a social or world peace. The message accents interior peace as the spiritual fruit of greater faith, prayer, fasting, penance, and conversion. This is simply stated in an interview with Mirjana:

> *Father Vlasic:* So the message of the Madonna is a message of peace?
>
> *Mirjana:* Yes. Primarily peace of soul. If a person has it in his soul, he is surrounded by it.

A message reported by Jelena conveys this same emphasis. At one point Jelena began reading a book that discussed the possible contents of the third secret from the Fatima apparitions in 1917. She became anxious and afraid over the thought of world punishments and wars. When Our Lady spoke to her later that day, her message was:

Do not think about wars, chastisements, evil. It is when you concentrate on these things that you are on the way to enter into them. Your responsibility is to accept divine peace; to live it.

Divine peace of soul will triumph over all possible temporal disorders, including the chastisements contained in the ten secrets. Spiritual peace must be manifested in reconciliation among humanity. Thus prayer is an integral part of the call to peace:

Dear children, without prayer, there is no peace. Therefore, I say to you, dear children, pray at the foot of the cross for peace (Sept. 6, 1984).

The elements of world-wide, Christ-centered peace and the means to bring it about are evident in this early message from June 26, 1981:

Peace, peace, peace...nothing but peace. Men must be reconciled with God and with each other. For this to happen, it is necessary to believe, to pray, to fast, and to go to Confession. Go in God's peace.

Many townspeople and pilgrims at Medjugorje reported seeing the word "MIR," Croatian for peace, written in large letters in the sky on August 6, 1981. This phenomenon is part of the summons to peace, a sign in nature rather than a message in words.

The Madonna has identified herself as the "Queen of Peace," and has requested June 25to be a feast day honoring her as the Queen of Peace. Just as the title "Our Lady of the Rosary" summed up the Blessed Virgin's message at Fatima, the title "Queen of Peace" signifies the importance this theme has in the message of Medjugorje.

The peace of Christ comes from greater prayer, fasting, penance, and conversion. Interior peace is the foundation for family peace, social peace, and even world peace.

The Gospels urge us to accept the gift of Christ's peace into our hearts, a peace that is the goal of the Christian life.

Jesus describes peace as a serenity of heart that the world cannot give:

> Peace I leave with you; My peace I give
> to you; not as the world gives do I give it
> to you. Let not your hearts be troubled,
> neither let them be afraid (Jn 14:27).

It is significant that peace is the first word the Risen Christ spoke to His disciples. In the Gospel of John we read:

> Jesus came and stood among them and
> said to them: "Peace be with you."
> Jesus said to them again, "Peace be with
> you"…Jesus came and stood among them,
> and said, "Peace be with you" (Jn 20: 19-
> 20, 26).

During His public ministry, Christ gave His gift
of peace to individuals often in connection with miracles
and healings. This is evident in the healing of the woman
with a hemorrhage: "Daughter, your faith has made you
well, go in peace, and be healed of your disease" (Mk 5:
34); and in the pardon of Christ to the penitent woman
who anointed Him: "And He said to the woman, 'Your
faith has saved you; go in peace'" (Lk 7:50).

The gift of peace seems to have entered the world
from the very moment of Christ's birth, as proclaimed by
the multitude of angels in their Christmas praise: "Glory
to God in the highest, and on earth peace among men
with whom He is pleased" (Lk 2:17).

The disciples were to bring the gift of peace to
those with open hearts:

> Whatever house you enter, first say,
> "Peace be to this house!" And if a son of
> peace is there, your peace shall rest upon
> him; but if not, it shall return to you (Lk
> 10: 5-6).

The individual's peace should even surpass that of family, of community, and of society. The peacemakers are praised in the Beatitudes for bringing about social peace (Mt 5:9); Christ proclaims the need for the "salt of the earth" to remain in peace among themselves (Mk 9: 50).

The peace the Christian experiences in this world is a foreshadowing of the ultimate peace to be experienced in the glory of eternal life. The Canticle of Zechariah points to peace as the goal for those followers of the Lord who will "...give light to those who sit in darkness and the shadow of death, to guide our feet into the way of peace" (Lk 1:79).

Yet, the Gospels state that not all will accept the peace of Christ. As Jesus neared the city of Jerusalem, he wept in sorrow for those who refused to accept His message of peace Their rejection of Christ and His way of peace eventually led to the destruction of Jerusalem. Our own generation would do well to reflect upon the sorrowful words of Jesus, "Would that even today you know the things that make for peace" (Lk 19: 41).

Despite the turmoil of the world, Christ assures His followers of His final victory over earthly tribulation through the peace found only in Him:

> I have said this to you, that in Me you may have peace. In the world you have tribulation; but be of good cheer, I have overcome the world (Jn 16: 33).

Peace as a divine gift from Christ, peace as a goal of the Christian life, and social peace as a result of interior peace — are all present in the Gospels. There is a notable conformity to the Gospel in the message of peace attributed to "Mary, Queen of Peace." It is evident that the way the message of Medjugorje speaks of faith, prayer, fasting, penance, conversion, and peace is solidly grounded in the heart of Sacred Scripture.

It is also worthy of note that the Medjugorjian message seems to be a calling for a return to the more committed ascetical practices of the early Church. This is seen, for example, in the request for Wednesday and Friday fasts. Certainly the fiber of Christian living in the first centuries of the faith, in generosity of prayer and penance, stands as a convicting example for contemporary Christians who have discarded these ascetical practices. The eternal truths of the Gospel decisively dispel any notion that the authentic Christian life can be bereft of committed faith, prayer, fasting, penance, conversion and peace.

Chapter III

In the Heart of the Church

Peace through faith, fasting, penance and conversion are only part of what Our Lady is saying to the Church and the world in these apparitions. The Madonna has also specified ways they are to be lived out in the daily life of the Christian. Flowering from the foundation themes are developmental themes which help the believer to understand fully and implement the message of Medjugorje in a deeper way.

The devotional themes focus on two areas: doctrinal elements and devotional practices. In this chapter we will discuss the doctrinal elements of the roles of Jesus Christ and the Blessed Virgin; the Holy Spirit; the Sacred and Immaculate Hearts; sin, Satan, heaven, hell and purgatory; and the signs of the times. We will look at these themes first as they are manifest in the message of Medjugorje and then in comparison with the conciliar and post-conciliar documents of the Church.

The One Mediator Jesus Christ

The message of Medjugorje is, above all, Christ centered. Jesus as the redeemer of humanity and His sole role as the mediator for all people to the heavenly Father is stressed whether the Madonna is requesting greater devotion "to my Son," prayer for the "victory of Jesus," or atonement for offenses committed against the "Heart of my Son." Jesus Christ as the very source of salvation is clearly stated in the message given in January 1982: "My Son suffered on the cross. He redeemed the world on the cross. Salvation comes from the cross." The role of Christ as the sole mediator to the Father appears in the message: "In God's eyes, there are no divisions and no religions. You in the world have made the divisions. The one mediator is Jesus Christ."

Our Lady directs believers toward her Son both in faith and in prayer: "Please pray to Jesus. I am His Mother and I intercede for you to Him. But all your prayers go to Jesus." On several occasions she has appeared with Jesus, either as a child or in His Passion, and has stated, "Do whatever He tells you." These are also her words at the wedding feast at Cana (Jn. 2:4).

The role of Jesus Christ as redeemer of humanity and as sole mediator of the world to the Father is unquestionably present in the documents of the Second Vatican Council.

Sacrosanctum Concilium (Constitution on the Sacred Liturgy) begins by referring to Jesus Christ as "the Mediator between God and Man" (S.C., No. 5).

The opening line of the encyclical **Redemptor Hominis** offers this simple but profound statement: "The Redeemer of Man, Jesus Christ, is the center of the universe and of history" (R.H., No. 5). Pope John Paul II connects the fundamental mission of the Church with the proclamation of Jesus Christ, the source of salvation:

> Our response must be: Our spirit is set in one direction. The only direction for our intellect, will and heart is towards Him, Christ, the Redeemer of Man. We wish to look towards Him because there is salvation in no one but Him, the Son of God . . . (R.H., No. 7)

The centrality of Christ in the message of Medjugorje is an authentic echo of the Church's faith and teaching as seen in these documents.

Pray to the Holy Spirit That He May Descend

Renewal in the Holy Spirit is strongly encouraged in the messages. Our Lady has directed the parish of St. James to pray for a greater outpouring of the Holy Spirit and to seek frequently His guidance and intervention. Our Lady called for a novena in preparation for Pentecost in June 1984. These messages reflect aspects of the Holy Spirit's role in the Church:

> The important thing is to pray to the Holy Spirit that He may descend. When you have Him, you have everything.

People make a mistake when they turn only to the saints for everything (October 21, 1983).

. . . Pray for the Spirit of Truth, especially you from the parish. You need the Spirit of Truth in order to convey the messages the way they are, without adding to them or taking away anything; the way I gave them to you. Pray that the Holy Spirit may inspire you with the spirit of prayer (June 9, 1984).

Be occupied with the one thing necessary, and let yourselves be guided by the Holy Spirit. Then your work will go well (July 14, 1983).

The focus of the Medjugorjian message is a renewed sense of the vital presence of the Holy Spirit both in the individual's life and in the universal Church. The outpouring of the Holy Spirit is a time of abundant graces, as is stated in the message of May 9, 1985:

Dear children, you do not know how many graces God is giving you. These days when the Holy Spirit is working in a special way, you do not want to advance, your hearts are turned towards earthly things, and you are occupied by them. Turn your hearts to prayer and ask

that the Holy Spirit be poured upon you.
Thank you for your response to my call.

The role of the Holy Spirit in the birth, mission, and spiritual revitalization of the Church is an essential doctrine of the Church. **Lumen Gentium** (Dogmatic Constitution on the Church) attests to the role of the Holy Spirit in the continual sanctification of the Church, the indwelling of the Holy Spirit in the hearts of the faithful, the bestowal of various hierarchical and charismatic gifts, and the instant renewal of the Church through the Holy Spirit (L.G., No. 4).

The need for unceasing prayer and renewal in the Holy Spirit called for at Medjugorje appears in the 1979 exhortation by Pope John Paul II, **Cathechesi tradendae** (Cathechesis in Our Time). The Holy Father discusses the work of the Holy Spirit in the effort of every catechist, and points to the norms and goal of the authentic "renewal in the Spirit":

> To invoke the Spirit constantly, to be in communion with Him, to endeavor to know His authentic inspirations must be the attitude of the teaching Church and of every catechist.
>
> Secondly, the deep desire to understand better the Spirit's action and to entrust himself to Him more fully . . . must bring about a catechetical awakening. For

"renewal in the Spirit" will be authentic and will have real fruitfulness in the Church, not so much according as it gives rise to the extraordinary charism, but according as it leads the greatest number of the faithful, as they travel their daily paths, to make a humble and patient and persevering effort to know the mystery of Christ better and better, and to bear witness to it (C.T., No 72).

The Holy Spirit's role in the Church as sanctifier, renewer and teacher has received considerable contemporary attention in the Church, an emphasis supported by the message of Medjugorje.

I, Your Mother, Love You All . . .

"I am the Blessed Virgin Mary . . . I want to be with you and to convert and reconcile all people." This message from the third day of the apparitions summarizes Mary's role on the Medjugorjian event. Our Lady as intercessor, mediatrix of all graces, and as loving mother of all humanity who longs to reconcile all people to God are key elements in understanding her message.

Her role as intercessor is evident in many different ways throughout the apparitions. She offers prayer and atonement to her Son for the countless sins of mankind as on the Feast of the Immaculate Conception in 1981 when she said, "My beloved Son, please forgive these numerous sins with which humanity is offending You."

Mary's role as "mediatrix," or secondary mediator, of the grace Christ merited on the cross is referred to in the Thursday Message of May 17, 1984: "My Son wishes to bestow on you special graces through me."

Our Lady as mediatrix of all graces is referred to in the June 19, 1986 message:

> Dear children, in these days, the Lord has allowed me to intercede for more graces for you...With these graces, dear children, I want your sufferings to be for you a joy. I am your Mother and I want to help you.

Our Lady is also the loving mother of humanity who sees all people of the world as her children whether or not they acknowledge her as their mother. Her love for us far surpasses our understanding of it, as the message reveals: "Dear children, if you only knew how great my love is for you, you would cry with joy."

Love is the basis for her appearance in Medjugorje and for the call to penance and prayer for the conversion of sinners:

> Dear children, I, your Mother, love you all. I love you even when you are far from

me and my Son. Dear children, I desire
the whole world to become my children,
but they are not willing. I want to give
them everything. Pray, therefore (May
24, 1984).

On November 14, 1985:

I wish to urge you to prayer...I feel pain
for everyone who has gone astray. But I
am a Mother and I forgive easily, and I
rejoice for every child who comes back
to me!

Mary's role as mother and intercessor for all her
earthly children has been a theme in many magisterial
documents such as this passage from **Lumen Gentium**
(No. 62):

Taken up into Heaven, she did not lay
aside this saving office but by her manifold
intercession continues to bring us the gifts
of eternal salvation. Therefore, the Blessed
Virgin is invoked in the Church under
the title of Advocate, Helper, Benefactress
and Mediatrix. This, however, is so
understood that it neither takes away
from nor adds anything to the dignity and
efficacy of Christ, the Mediator.

In the apostolic exhortation, **Marialis Cultus** (To Honor Mary, February 2, 1974) Pope Paul VI points to Mary's role of spiritual motherhood as the path to Christian unity:

> ...so today her intercession can help to bring to realization the time when the disciples of Christ will again find full communion in faith...the cause of Christian unity "properly pertains to the role of Mary's spiritual Motherhood" (M.C., No. 33).

The World Day of Peace, instituted by Pope Paul VI in **Marialis Cultus**, is celebrated on January 1st, the Feast of Mary, the Mother of God. The Pope speaks of the unity of these two themes — Mary, the Mother of God, and Peace — and urges the faithful to a renewed adoration of Christ, the "Prince of Peace," who offers his gift to people through Mary, "Queen of Peace."

> It is likewise a fitting occasion for renewing adoration to the newborn Prince of Peace, for listening once more to the glad tidings of the angels (cf. Lk 2: 14), and for imploring from God through the Queen of Peace, the supreme gift of peace (M.C., No. 5).

Pope John Paul II emphasizes Mary's role as mediatrix in **Redemptoris Mater**, his 1987 Marian encyclical:

> She also has that specifically maternal role of mediatrix of mercy at His final coming, when all those who belong to Christ shall be made alive, when the last enemy to be destroyed is death (1 Cor. 15:26).

Consecrate Yourself Totally

Devotion to the Sacred Heart of Jesus and the Immaculate Heart of Mary, traditional devotions in the Church, have also been encouraged in the messages. The focus on consecration of individuals and families, veneration of the wounds of Christ, and reparation and atonement for the unceasing sins of humanity also reflect the essential elements of ecclesiastically-approved devotions.

Jelena has received several messages that call for a consecration of each family to the Sacred Heart, of total consecration to the Immaculate Heart, as well as specific prayers of consecration.

"Pray, three hours a day...You pray too little... Consecrate five minutes to the Sacred Heart; every family is its image" (June 28, 1983). "Consecrate yourself totally to the Immaculate Heart. Abandon yourselves totally. I will protect you…" On October 20, 1983, the message was given: "All families should consecrate themselves to the Sacred Heart every day."

Reparation and atonement to the Sacred Heart of Jesus for the unceasing sins of humanity were also requested of the parishioners later in the same Lenten season:

> This evening I am especially asking you to venerate the Heart of my Son, Jesus. Make atonement for the wounds inflicted on the heart of my Son. That heart has been offended by all sorts of sins.

Furthermore, devotion to the Sacred Heart is highly recommended because of the worthy adoration and reparation offered to Jesus Christ and its close association with the Eucharist. Pope Paul VI stated that this devotion fulfills the purpose of popular devotion sought by Vatican II (**Sacrosanctum Concilium**, n. 13), in a unique way.

On December 8th, during the 1983 Holy Year of Redemption, Pope John Paul II issued a family prayer of consecration to the Sacred Heart and the Immaculate Heart. He also formally consecrated the world to the Immaculate Heart of Mary on the Feast of the Annunciation, March 25, 1984.

In **Reconcilitio et Paenitenti**a (On Reconcili-ation and Penance, December 2, 1984) the Pontiff invites the faithful to turn to the Heart of Christ, to foster a greater hatred of sin, and to seek greater conversion to God, our source of peace and reconciliation. This parallels the specific Medjugorjian themes of faith, conversion, peace and repentance:

> I invite you all to join me in turning to Christ's Heart, the eloquent sign of Divine Mercy, the "propitiation for our sins," "our peace and reconciliation," that we may draw from it an interior encouragement to hate sin and to be converted to God, and find it in the divine kindness which lovingly responds to human repentance (R.P., No. 33).

The Holy Father then directs the faithful to the Immaculate Heart of Mary:

> Into the hands of this Mother...to her Immaculate Heart — to which we have repeatedly entrusted the whole of humanity, disturbed by sin and tormented by so many tensions and conflicts — I now in a special way entrust the intention: that through her intercession humanity may discover and travel the path of penance, the only path that can lead it to full reconciliation (R.P., No. 35).

It is evident that there is a striking similarity between the themes of these encyclicals and the Medjugorjian messages reported in the same contemporary time frame.

Heaven, Purgatory, Hell and Satan

The existence of heaven, purgatory and hell as real states of life which exist after earthly death, and the real and aggressive efforts of Satan in spiritual warfare today are brought out in the Madonna's message.

The six visionaries have all reported to have seen heaven. Those who did not ask to be spared the experience were also shown purgatory and hell. When they say purgatory, Our Lady said, "Those people are waiting for your prayers and sacrifices."

Mirjana was asked by Father Tomislav Vlasic in 1983 whether many people go to hell in this day and age. Mirjana responded: "I asked her about that recently, and she said that today most people go to purgatory, the next greatest go to hell, and only a few go directly to heaven."

Mirjana describes purgatory as having different levels, some closer to hell and other high and closer to heaven. "Most people," she said, "think many souls are released from purgatory into heaven on All Saints' Day, but most souls are taken into heaven on Christmas Day."

Satan's attempts to counteract the plans of Our Lady is a Medjugorjian theme that is repeated with intensity as these two messages indicate: "Satan is continually trying to thwart my plans. Pray with your heart, and in your prayer, give yourselves entirely to Jesus" (August 11, 1984). And "...Satan is working even more violently to take away the joy from each one of you. Through prayer, you can totally disarm him and ensure happiness" (January 24, 1985).

Satan appeared unexpectedly to Mirjana in 1982. She rejected him. Immediately the Virgin arrived and Satan disappeared. Then the Blessed Virgin gave her the following message, in substance:

> Excuse me for this, but you must realize that Satan exists. One day he appeared before the throne of God and asked permission to submit the Church to a period of trial. God gave him permission to try the Church for one century. This century is under the power of the devil, but when the secrets confided to you come to pass, his power will be destroyed. Even now he is beginning to lose his power and has become aggressive. He is destroying marriages, creating divisions among priest, and is responsible for obsessions and murder. You must protect yourselves against these things through

fasting and prayer, especially community prayer. Carry blessed objects with you. Put them in your house, and restore the use of holy water.

In a letter to the Holy Father in 1983, Father Tomislav Vlasic further explains what took place:

> According to certain Catholic experts who have studied these apparitions, the message of Mirjana may shed light on the vision Pope Leo XIII had. According to them, it was after having had an apocalyptic vision of the future of the Church that Leo XIII introduced the prayer to St. Michael which priests used to recite after Mass up to the time of the Second Vatican Council. These experts say that the century of trials foreseen by Leo XIII is about to end.

The same afterlife realities are attested to in **The Reality of Life After Death**, issued May 29, 1979, by the Sacred Congregation for the Doctrine of the Faith. Because of contemporary confusion over these doctrines, the document unambiguously states the reality of heaven and hell, and the possible need of souls to enter purgatory:

In fidelity to the New Testament and Tradition, the Church believes in the happiness of the just who will one day be with Christ. She believes that there will be one eternal punishment for the sinner, who will be deprived of the sight of God, and that this punishment will have a repercussion on the whole reality of the sinner. She believes in the possibility of a purification for the elect before they see God, a purification altogether different from the punishment of the damned.

These truths are also stated by Pope Paul VI in **The Credo of the People of God** (June 20, 1968).

The document, **Christian Faith and Demonology,** is the summary of the teaching of the Church on Satan and his activity. It affirms the reality of the devil and the need consciously and actively to defend ourselves from his efforts:

When a doubt is thrown these days on the reality of the devil we must, as we observed earlier, look to the constant and universal teaching of the Church and to its chief source, the teaching of Christ. It is in the teaching of the Gospel and in the heart of the faith as lived that the existence of the world of demons is revealed as a dogma.

This document also speaks of the importance of faith in winning victory over the devil through prayer:

> Faith tells us that evil is a "living, spiritual being that is perverted and perverts others...Faith opens the heart of prayer. Wherein it finds its triumph and crown, for prayer wins for us the victory over evil, thanks to God's grace.

It is evident that the message of Medjugorje is in complete conformity with traditional Church teaching regarding Satan, heaven, hell and purgatory.

The Signs of the Times

There is a sense of urgency in the Blessed Virgin's call for immediate conversion because of her prediction of worldwide calamities in the near future. This extract from the letter sent to Pope John Paul II states that the time for conversion following the chastisement will be brief:

> After the first admonition, the others will follow in a rather short time. Thus people will have some time for conversion.

After the visible sign appears, those who are still alive will have little time for conversion. For that reason, the Blessed Virgin invites us to urgent conversation and reconciliation.

Mirjana gave the same imperative to immediate conversion, warning us all to prepare spiritually for the future. She said:

Yes, prepare! The Madonna said people should prepare themselves spiritually, be ready, and not panic; be reconciled in their souls. They should be ready for the worst, to die tomorrow. They should accept God now so that they will not be afraid. No one accepts death easily, but they can be at peace with their souls if they are believers.

According to the visionaries, the apparitions of Our Lady at Medjugorje are the last series of apparitions on earth:

Mirjana: She said that she stayed with us for a long time, longer than is necessary, but that this is the last apparition on earth...

Father Vlasic: What do you mean, "the last apparition on earth?"

Mirjana: It is the last time Jesus or Mary will appear on earth.

Father Vlasic: What do you mean "appear?"

Mirjana: The last time they will appear as they have so that you can speak with them.

Father Vlasic: You mean that this is the last apparition in this era, in this period of the Church, or that they will never again come to earth?

Mirjana: I don't know. The Madonna said this is the last apparition on earth.

The Blessed Virgin is urgent in her plea for immediate conversion as the message from the spring of 1983 shows:

Hasten your conversion. Do not wait for the sign that has been announced for the unbelievers; it will already be too late for them to have a conversion. You who believe, be converted and deepen your faith.

Both the reference to a serious upcoming world chastistment that is to take place within the lifetime of the visionaries and the claim that this is the last appearance of the Blessed Virgin Mary on earth accentuate the serious nature of her message of conversion, reconciliation and spiritual preparation.

However, the message of Medjugorje is pre-eminently a message of peace, not disaster. Peace is the heart of the message: the peace of Christ within the soul of the believer will triumph over any temporal disorder which may await humanity. It is this peace that Our Lady refers to in this message to Jelena:

> Do not think about wars, chastisements, evil. It is when you concentrate on these things that you are on your way to enter into them. Your responsibility is to accept divine peace, to live it.

The post-conciliar teachings of the Magisterium also reflect a pressing concern for the conversion of all mankind. **Redemptor Hominis** clearly states the increasing threat to man by the works of his hands and mind which results in an atmosphere of fear:

All too soon, and often in an unforeseeable
way, this manifold activity of man…turns
against man himself…Man therefore lives
increasingly in fear (R.H., No. 15).

Man's material advancements are praiseworthy
but can be a means to self-domination and manipulation
by his disregard for God's sovereignity (R.H., No. 16).
This statement is quite similar to Mary's description
of the West, "The West has advanced in civilization,
but without God, as though it were its own creator"
(undated, July – December, 1981).

The Church's responsibility to pray for God's
mercy on the world, especially at this point in history,
is expressed in Dives in Misericordia (On the Mercy of
God, 1980):

"…however, at no time and in no
historical period **especially at a
moment as critical as our own**
— can the Church forget the prayer that
is a cry for the mercy of God amid the
many forms of evil which weigh upon
humanity and threaten it" (D.M., No.
15). (author's emphasis)

Pope John Paul II further states that it is faith and
hope in God that urge him to implore God's mercy on
humanity which is "threatened by an immense danger":

And if any of our contemporaries does not share the faith and hope which lead me, as a servant of Christ and steward of the mysteries of God, to implore God's mercy for humanity in our present hour of history, let him at least try to understand the reason for my concern. It is dictated by love for man, for all that is human and which, according to the intuitions of many of our contemporaries, is threatened by an immense danger" (D.M., No. 15).

Reconciliatio et Paenitentia, in the words of St. Peter, exhorts the faithful to that unity, zeal and willingness to suffer — "if it should be God's will" — necessary to combat evil at this critical moment:

At an hour of history which is no less critical, I dare to join my exhortation to that of the Prince of the Apostles, the first to occupy this See of Rome as a witness to Christ and as a Pastor of the Church... "Have unity of spirit...Be zealous for what is right." And he added: "It is better to suffer for doing right, if that should be God's will, than for doing wrong" (R.P., No. 35).

Chapter IV

Living the Messages

The message of Medjugorje is practical and pastoral in nature. Though theologically sound and in complete conformity with Church teaching, its primary purpose is not to be studied but to make a difference in an individual's life. The Blessed Virgin Mary has not revealed astonishing supernatural realities or new aspects of her role as mediatrix or intercessor but rather, as a loving mother, she repeatedly returns to the ordinary ways believers can live out their faith. The next set of themes are the "how-tos" of the messages. They develop the foundational themes of faith, prayer, fasting, penance, conversion and peace in a way that they can be lived out day by day. We will consider them in the light of contemporary Church documents to grasp the significance of Mary's message and their conformity to Church teaching.

The Mass is the Greatest Prayer

The message of Medjugorje calls for a strong devotion to Jesus Christ truly present in the Holy

Eucharist. The May 30, 1984, message encourages daily Mass attendance:

> Children, I want the Holy Mass to be the gift of the day for you. Go to it; long for it to begin, because Jesus Christ Himself gives Himself to you during Mass. So, live for this moment when you are purified. Pray much that the Holy Spirit will renew your parish. If people assist at Mass in a half-hearted fashion, they will return with cold, empty hearts.

The Mass, as the continuation of the sacrifice of Jesus Christ at Calvary, is the summit of prayer and worship of God:

> The Mass is the greatest prayer from God, and you will never understand the greatness of it. Therefore, you must be perfect and humble at Mass, and you must prepare for it.

Adoration of the Blessed Sacrament is stressed as a time when great graces are received:

> Adore continually the Most Holy Sacrament of the Altar. I am always

present when the faithful are in adoration.
Then special graces are being received.

The Madonna has called for a renewal of Mass attendance, including the "very young" of each family: ". . . encourage the very young to pray and to go to Holy Mass." Perseverance in attending Mass despite hard weather will bring about the Lord's abundant reward (November 2, 1985). But mere attendance without whole-hearted participation is not enough:

> Dear children, I am calling you to more attentive prayer and participation in the Mass. I wish you to experience God within yourselves during Mass (May 16, 1985).

The Blessed Virgin summons all the faithful to live the Mass throughout the day:

> There are many of you who have experienced the beauty of the Mass, but there are some who come unwillingly. I have chosen you, dear children, and Jesus is giving you His graces in the Holy Mass.
>
> Therefore, live consciously the Holy Mass. Let every coming to Holy

Mass be joyful. Come with love and accept the Holy Mass (April 3, 1986).

The Constitution on the Sacred Liturgy **(Sacrosanctum Concilium)** strongly emphasizes full and complete participation in the Mass by all Christians in the fullness of faith:

> They (the faithful) should be instructed by God's word, and be nourished at the table of the Lord's Body. They should give thanks to God, offering the Immaculate Victim, not only through the hands of the priest but also together with him; they should learn to offer themselves through Christ, the Mediator. They should be drawn day by day into ever more perfect union with God and each other, so that finally God may be all in all (S.C., No. 48).

Inaestimabile Donum (Instruction on Certain Norms Concerning the Worship of the Eucharistic Mystery, April, 1980) repeats traditional Church teaching regarding adoration of the Blessed Sacrament:

> Public and private devotion to the Holy Eucharist outside Mass also is highly recommended: For the presence of

Christ, who is adored by the faithful in
the Sacrament, derives from the sacrifice
and is directed towards sacramental and
spiritual communion (I.D., No. 20).

Pope John Paul II describes the unequaled
earthly union with Christ attainable in the reception
of the Sacrament of Holy Eucharist in the encyclical
Redemptor Hominis:

The Eucharist is the most perfect
Sacrament of this union. By celebrating
and also partaking of the Eucharist we
unite ourselves with Christ on earth
and in Heaven . . . but we always do
so through the redeeming act of His
sacrifice . . . (R.H., No. 20).

I Wish to Call You to Confession

The request for sacramental Confession has been
present since the third day of the apparitions, June 26,
1981, and as such is integral to the message of Medjugorje
as a major means of conversion.

Reconciliation with God and with neighbor is
effected by the Sacrament of Penance:

Men must be reconciled with God and
with one another. For this to happen, it is

necessary to believe, to pray, to fast, **and
to go to confession**.

Our Lady has referred to the Sacrament of
Penance as a "medicine for the Church of the West,"
stating that "whole regions of the Church would be
healed if believers would go to Confession once a
month."

Mary's request for monthly Confession was made
at least as early as August 6, 1982, and was immediately
implemented by the members of St. James parish. On
November 7, 1983, Our Lady spoke to Jelena and warned
against a type of mechanical, habitual Confession:

> Don't go to Confession from habit to stay
> the same after it. No, that is not good.
> Confession should give drive to your
> faith. It should stir you, and draw you
> near to Jesus. If Confession doesn't mean
> much to you, you will be converted only
> with difficulty.

Confession as a means of surrender to God is the
focus of the message given on the eve of the Feast of the
Annunciation, March 25, 1985:

> Dear children, today I wish to call you to
> Confession, even if you had Confession
> a few days ago. I wish you to experience

my Feast Day within yourselves. You cannot, unless you give yourselves to God completely. And so I am calling you to reconciliation with God! Thank you for your response to my call.

The Church's Magesterium has stressed the importance of sacramental Confession as the forgiveness of sin and reconciliation with Christ several times since Vatican II. In 1974, the document **Misericordiam Suam** introduced the New Order of Penance and spoke of the significance of sacramental Confession, in particular for the forgiveness of grave sin:

> Those who depart from the fellowship of the love of God through grave sin are recalled through the Sacrament of Penance to the life which they had lost. Those who fall into venial sin, however, experiencing their weakness daily, receive through frequent Confession the strength to arrive at the full freedom of the Children of God.
>
> . . . in order to receive the saving remedy of the Sacrament of Penance, the Christian should confess to a priest all and every grave sin which he can recall after an examination of his conscience (M.S., No. 7).

Reconciliatio et Paenitentia emphasizes that sacramental confession is to be the regular and ordinary means to receive the forgiveness of sins and should not be disregarded.

> The first conviction is that, for a Christian, the Sacrament of Penance is the ordinary way of obtaining forgiveness and the remission of serious sins committed after Baptism . . . In the school of faith we learn that the same Savior desired and provided that the simple and precious Sacraments of faith would ordinarily be the effective means through which His redemptive power passes and operates. It would therefore be foolish, as well as presumptuous, to wish arbitrarily to disregard the means of grace and salvation which the Lard has provided (R.P., No. 31).

The Holy Father also refers to the contemporary neglect of the Sacrament and calls for renewal and reaffirmation:

> It is good to renew and reaffirm this faith [in the Sacrament of Penance] at the moment when it might be weakening, losing some of its completeness, or

entering into an area of shadow or silence, threatened as it is by the negative elements in the above mentioned crisis. For the Sacrament of Confession is indeed being undermined . . . A further negative influence is the routine of a sacramental practice sometimes lacking in fervor and real spontaneity, deriving perhaps from a mistaken and distorted idea of the effects of the Sacrament. It is therefore appropriate to recall the principal aspects of this great sacrament (R.P., No. 28).

With Rosaries in your Hand you will Conquer

The rosary is unquestionably the fundamental form of devotional prayer requested in the Medjugorjian message. Our Lady often requested that the rosary be prayed more frequently.

On the eve of the Feast of the Assumption, August 14, 1984, Ivan reported an unexpected apparition of Mary accompanied with the request for the full fifteen-decade rosary every day: "I ask the people to pray with me these days. Pray all the more . . . Say every day at least one rosary; joyful, sorrowful and glorious mysteries."

The Madonna specifically requested a nightly family rosary in two Thursday Messages (September 27, 1984 and October 8, 1984) for the fulfillment of her plans for the parish and for all people.

On June 25, 1985, four years after the apparitions began, Our Lady asked everyone to pray the rosary in order to combat Satan:

> Dear children, I ask you to ask everyone to pray the rosary. With the rosary you will overcome all the troubles which Satan is trying to inflict on the Catholic Church.

On August 8, 1985, Our Lady reiterated the powerful effect of the rosary against Satan:

> Dear Children, today I call you to pray against Satan in a special way. Satan wants to work more now that you know he is active. Dear children, put on your armor against Satan; with rosaries in your hands you will conquer. Thank you for your response to my call.

Our Lady gave this message to Mirjana when she asked, "Madonna, what do you wish to say to priests?": "Let all priests pray the rosary. Give time to the rosary" (June 25, 1985).

Finally, in the June 12, 1986 message, the Madonna begs that the rosary be prayed with commitment and lively faith so we may understand the reason for her apparitions:

Today I am begging you to pray the rosary with lively faith. Only this way can I help you. Pray. I cannot help you because you don't want to be moved. Dear children, I am calling you to pray the rosary. The rosary should be your commitment, prayed with joy and so you will understand why I am visiting you for such a long time. I want to teach you to pray.

In **Marialis Cultus**, Pope Paul VI extols the benefits of frequent recitation of the rosary:

To this our predecessors have devoted close attention and care. On many occasions they have recommended its frequent recitation, encouraged its diffusion, explained its nature, recognized its suitability for fostering contemplative prayer — prayer of both praise and petition — and recalled its intrinsic effectiveness for promoting Christian life and apostolic commitment (M.C., No. 42).

Paul VI continues to describe the rosary as a meditational prayer on the principal salvation events accomplished by Christ and the final events in the life of Our Lady, and as such it is "the compendium of the entire Gospels" (M.C., No. 45). The rosary is a Gospel prayer of continual praise of Christ. It is Jesus who is the object of the Angel's announcement and the greeting of Elizabeth; therefore, the rosary is intrinsically Christ-centered.

> As Gospel prayer, centered on the mystery of the redemptive Incarnation, the rosary is therefore a prayer with a clearly Christological orientation. Its most characteristic element, in fact, the litany-like succession of Hail Marys, becomes in itself an unceasing praise of Christ, who is the ultimate object both of the Angel's announcement and of the greeting of the mother of John the Baptist: "Blessed is the fruit of your womb" (Lk. 1:42) (M.C., No. 46).

Pope John Paul II's **Familiaris Consortio** particularly encourages the recitation of the family rosary, another call accentuated in the message of Medjugorje:

> We now desire, as a continuation of the thought of our predecessors, to recommend strongly the recitation of the family rosary . . . There is no doubt that .

.. the rosary should be considered as one of the best and most efficacious prayers in common that the Christian family is invited to recite. We like to think, and sincerely hope, that when the family gathering becomes a time of prayer, the rosary is a frequent and favored manner of praying (F.C., No. 42).

The Answer is in the Gospel

Reading and praying the Sacred Scriptures are integral components in the Blessed Virgin's message. According to Jelena, Our Lady has responded on several occasions, "Why so many questions? The answer is in the Gospel." Our Lady requested that Matthew 6:24-34 be read every Thursday during the parish service. The messages reaffirm that the Scriptures are a source of spiritual strength, an encouragement to pray, and are the divinely revealed Word of God. This message given to Jelena accents the daily strength that comes from reading the Bible:

I will tell you a spiritual secret: If you wish to be stronger than evil, make an active conscience for yourself — that is, pray a reasonable amount in the morning; read a text of the Holy Scripture and plant the divine word in your heart; and try to live it during the day, especially in moments of trial — so you will be stronger than evil.

The emphasis on reading and praying Sacred Scripture is the theme in this Thursday Message to the parish:

Dear children, today I ask you to read the Bible in your houses every day and let it be in a visible place in the house, so that it will always encourage you to pray.

A renewal of Sacred Scripture in prayer, study and meditation has been emphasized by the Magisterium. **Dei Verbum** (the Dogmatic Constitution on Divine Revelation) discusses the central role of Sacred Scripture in the Church as inerrent and as the norm of faith for the believer:

She [the Church] has always regarded, and continues to regard the Scripture, taken together with Sacred Tradition, as the supreme rule of her faith. For, since they are inspired by God and committed to writing once and for all time, they present God's own Word in an unalterable form, and they make the voice of the Holy Spirit sound again and again in the words of the prophets and apostles. It follows that . . . the entire Christian religion should be nourished and be ruled by Sacred Scripture . . . (D.V., No. 21, 22).

Dei Verbum also attests to the primacy of the Gospels among all inspired writings, which the Medjugorjian messages also emphasize:

It is common knowledge that among all the inspired writings, even among those of the New Testament, the Gospels have special place, and rightly so, because they are our principal source for the life and teaching of the Incarnate Word, our Savior (D.V., No. 18).

The Sacred Congregation for Religious and Secular Institutes issued an invitation that Medjugorje echoes in its 1981 document, **La Plenaria** (The Contemplative Dimension of Religious Life):

Listening to and meditating on the Work of God is a daily encounter with the "surpassing knowledge of Jesus Christ" (PC 6; ES II, 16, 1). The Council "warmly and insistently exhorts all the Christian faithful, especially those who live the religious life, to learn this sublime knowledge" (DV 25) (L.P., No. 8).

The Power of Love

Love of neighbor and the concern for the conversion and well-being of our neighbor is the heart of fraternal charity. It is fundamental to Christianity and to the Medjugorjian message. Love of one's neighbor and family is linked to the power of intercession as in this message:

> Dear children, again I invite you to prayer of the heart. If you pray from your heart, dear children, the ice cold hearts of your brothers will be melted and every barrier will disappear. Conversion will be easily achieved by those who want it. You must intercede for this gift for your neighbors" (January 23, 1986).

And the Thursday Message of May 29, 1986, calls for love of God and neighbor, a living in mutual love:

> Dear children, today I am calling you to a life of love towards God and your neighbor. Without love, dear children, you cannot do anything. Therefore, dear children, I am calling you to live in

mutual love. Only in that way can you love me and accept everyone around you coming to your parish. Everyone will feel my love through you. Therefore, today I beg you to start loving with a burning love.

The "power of love" is the right response for one's enemies:

> Dear children, I am calling you to love your neighbors, to love those from whom the evil is coming to you, and so in the power of love you will be able to judge the intentions of the heart. Pray and love, dear children. In the power of love you can do even those things that seem impossible to you" (November 7, 1985).

This message given to Jelena is strongly evocative of the Sermon on the Mount: "Love your enemies. Pray for them and bless them."

Love of neighbor must first begin with love of family members, as the June 6, 1985, message states:

> Dear children, in these days many people of all nationalities will come to the parish, and now I am telling you to love. Love, first of all, members of your own family

> and then you might be able to accept in
> love all those who are coming. Thank
> you for your response to my call.

An authentic love of neighbor, including love of
enemies, is a fundamental Christian directive ratified by
Vatican II. **Apostolicam Actuositatem** (Decree on the
Apostolate of the Laity, November 18, 1965) speaks of
the love of neighbor as the personal commandment of
Christ:

> The greatest commandment of the law
> is to love God with one's whole heart
> and one's neighbor as oneself (cf. Mt.
> 22:37-40). Christ has made this love of
> neighbor His personal commandment
> and has enriched it with a new meaning
> when He willed Himself, along with His
> brothers, to be the object of His charity
> saying: "When you showed it to one of
> the least of My brothers here, you show it
> to Me" (Mt. 35:40) (A.A., No. 8).

The same document goes on to identify fraternal
charity as the distinguishing characteristic of Christian
discipleship:

> In assuming human nature He has
> united to Himself all humanity in a

supernatural solidarity which makes of it
a single family. He has made charity the
distinguishing mark of His disciples, in
the words: "By this will all men know
you for My disciples, by the love you bear
one another" (Jn. 13:35) (A.A., No. 8).

The Gospel call to "love your enemies," stated
so simply in the Medjugorjian content, is re-affirmed
in the **Pastoral Constitution on the Church in the
Modern World** (December 7, 1965):

The teaching of Christ even demands
that we forgive injury, and the precept of
love, which is the commandment of the
New Law, includes all our enemies (cf.
Mt. 5:43-44) (G.S., No 27).

"You in the World Have Made the Divisions"

The Medjugorjian theme of ecumenism stresses
cooperation between all peoples who worship the one
God and calls for a sincere respect for individuals with
different religious beliefs. The messages clearly state
the one and only mediator to the Father is Jesus Christ
and that one's own Church is not a matter of religious
indifference. Man has created religious differences
unintended by God. All religions are not equally filled
with the presence of the Holy Spirit; nor can they all

claim to be the one Church instituted by Jesus Christ. The visionaries tell us that the Madonna stated:

> In God's eyes, there are no divisions and there are no religions. You in the world have made the divisions. The one mediator is Jesus Christ. Which religion you belong to cannot be a matter of indifference. The presence of the Holy Spirit is not the same in every Church.

Mirjana expanded on this theme in an interview with Fr. Vlasic in 1983.

> She [the Madonna] also emphasized the failings of religious people, especially in small villages. For example, here in Medjugorje there is a separation between Serbians and Moslems. This separation is not good. The Madonna always stresses that there is but one God, and that people have enforced unnatural separation.

Mirjana questioned: If the Moslem religion is a good religion, what is the role of Jesus Christ? She responded,

> We did not discuss that. She merely explained and deplored the lack of

religious unity, "especially in the villages."
She said that everybody's religion should
be respected, and of course, one's own.

The conciliar document, **Nostrae Aetate**
(Declaration on the Relation of the Church to Non-
Christian Religions, October 28, 1965), sets forth
guidelines for Christian relations to non-Christian
religions. The Medjugorjian theme is remarkably similar
in content.

The Council Fathers first discuss the elements
of truth and high moral conduct that can be found in
several of the major world religions, then they turn to
the singularity of Christ and the completeness of the
Christian religion:

> The Catholic Church rejects nothing of
> what is true and holy in these religions.
> She has a high regard for the manner
> of life and conduct, the precepts and
> doctrines which, although differing
> in many ways from her own teaching,
> nevertheless often reflect a ray of that
> truth which enlightens all men. Yet,
> she proclaims and is in duty bound to
> proclaim without fail, Christ who is the
> way, the truth, and the life (Jn 1:6). In
> Him, in whom God reconciled all things
> to Himself (2 Cor 5:18-19), men find

the fullness of their religious life (N.A., No. 2).

The Magisterium consistently teaches that the Catholic Church is the one true Church of Christ. The fullness of the presence of the Holy Spirit, as alluded to in the Madonna's message, and the full means of His sanctification is found only in the Catholic Church as stated here in this passage from **Lumen Gentium**:

> This is the sole Church of Christ which in the Creed we profess to be one, holy, catholic and apostolic...This Church, constituted and organized as a society in the present world, subsists in the Catholic Church, which is governed by the successors of Peter and by the bishops in communion with him. Nevertheless, many elements of sanctification and of truth are found outside its visible confines. Since these are gifts belonging to the Church of Christ, they are forces impelling towards Catholic unity (L.G., No. 8).

Further, the post-conciliar document, **Ecumenical Collaboration at the Regional, National and Local Levels** (1975), stresses that ecumenical efforts are to be initiated by the "local Church" in every respective town or city:

> From the Catholic perspective ecumenical responsibilities of the local Church emerge clearly...Therefore, the local Church...can be in a very favorable position to make contact and establish fraternal relations with other Christian churches and communicate at these levels.

The Church is calling all parishes, whether urban or rural, to a greater respect, dialogue and prudent co-operation with other churches and with our separated brethren in Christ. The Church at the same time cautions the faithful to uphold and proclaim the fullness of the truth within the Catholic Church.

This commitment to the fullness of truth and yet tolerance and love for others is the same stance taken by the message of Medjugorje.

Let Family Prayer Take the First Place

Mary's message at Medjugorje promotes family prayer and community prayer as a powerful means of combating Satan in the modern world. The accent is on families united in prayer, but there is also a strong call for community prayer.

In addition to Mary's request that all Christians attend daily Mass, she has also requested the formation of prayer groups in all parishes:

> Yes, there is a need for a prayer group, not only in this parish, but in all parishes. Spiritual renewal is needed for the entire Church.

Communal, and especially family prayer is effective against Satan according to Mirjana:

> The devil is not in them [people in general] but they're under the influence of the devil. To prevent this, at least to some extent, the Madonna said we need communal prayer, family prayer. She stressed the need for family prayer most of all.

The ability and the degree to which families can pray together is greater than is commonly supposed, according to this dialogue between Jelena and the Madonna:

> *Madonna*: I know that every family can pray four hours a day.

Jelena: But if I tell this to the people, they may back out.

Madonna: Even you do not understand. It is only one-sixth of the day.

Jelena: I know that you want us to pray continually.

Everyone in the family is to participate in the life of prayer within the home:

Dear children, today I am calling you to prayer. You are forgetting that everyone is important, especially the elderly in the family. Incite them to pray. Let the youth be an example by their lives and testify for Jesus. Dear children, I beg you to start transforming yourselves through prayer and then you will know what you have to do (April 24, 1986).

This invitation is extended even to the youngest children:

Dear children, today I invite you to renew prayer in your families...Encourage the very young to pray and go to Holy Mass (March 7, 1985).

Furthermore, family prayer is to "take the first place in your families" (November 1, 1984). Family life is changed, is made "harmonious" through prayer:

> Dear children, I ask you to begin to change your life in your families. Let your family be a harmonious flower which I wish to give to Jesus. Dear children, every family should be active in prayer. It is my wish that the fruits of prayer will be seen one day in the family. Only that way will I give you as petals to Jesus in fulfillment of God's plan. Thank you for your response to my call (May 1, 1986).

A strong post-conciliar movement supported by the teaching of the Magisterium is reflected by the Medjugorjian stress on family and communal prayer. For example, the multiplication of youth prayer groups is noted by Pope John Paul II in **Catechesi Tradendae**:

> I may also mention the youth groups that, under varying names and forms but always with the purpose of making Jesus Christ known and of living the Gospel, are in some areas multiplying and flourishing in a sort of springtime that is very comforting to the Church...These

groups are a source of great hope for the Church of tomorrow (C.T., No. 47).

The Church recognizes the growth of small groups dedicated to communal prayer as a gift of God and encourages them to persevere in the 1978 document **Mutuae Relationes**:

> Today, by the disposition of divine providence, many of the faithful are led to gather into small groups to hear the Gospel, to meditate in depth and practice contemplation...It is indispensable to make certain that all, above all pastors, give themselves to prayer...(M.R., No. 16).

The apostolic exhortation **Familiaris Consortio** epitomizes the Magisterial teaching on the role of family prayer in a way that the message of Medjugorje parallels. The proper dignity and responsibility of the family can be achieved through joining in prayer:

> The dignity and responsibility of the Christian family as the domestic Church can be achieved only with God's unceasing aid, which will surely be granted if it is humbly and trustingly petitioned in prayer (F.C., No. 59).

The Holy Father exhorts the family to the family rosary and devotion to the Blessed Virgin Mary, quoting his predecessor Paul VI:

> "There is no doubt that...the rosary should be considered as one of the best and most efficacious prayers in common that the Christian family is invited to recite. We like to think and sincerely hope, that when the family gathering becomes a time of prayer, the rosary is a frequent and favoured manner of praying." In this way authentic devotion to Mary...constitutes a special instrument for nourishing loving communion in the family and for developing conjugal and family spirituality (F.C., No. 61).

Offer Every Sacrifice With Love

The patient endurance of trials and a willing acceptance of the unchangeable events in God's perfect will can be offered to God in reparation for the sins of mankind and for the conversion of sinners. This practice, deeply rooted in Catholic tradition, was one of the strongest themes from the apparitions of the Blessed Virgin Mary at Fatima in 1917. By "offering up" their sufferings and sacrifices the faithful "make up what is lacking in the sufferings of Christ" (Col 1:24) for the purification and sanctification of the Church. This theme is also strongly emphasized in Medjugorje.

A Thursday Message from the 1984 Lenten season illustrates the way we can share in the mystery of Christ's salvific death:

> Ponder how the Almighty is still suffering because of your sins. So when the sufferings come, offer them as your sacrifice to God.

This theme continues in the Thursday Message given October 11, 1984:

> Dear children, thank you for offering all your pains to God, even now when He is testing you through the fruits which you are reaping. Realize, dear children, that He loves you and for that reason He tests you. Always present your burdens to God and do not worry.

The "testing" was a long rain in the middle of the reaping season which caused great damage to the harvest.

This practice is praised by the Madonna in the message from July 4, 1985:

> Dear children, thank you for every sacrifice you have offered. Now I urge you to offer every sacrifice with love. I desire that you who are helpless begin with trust. The Lord will give to you always if you trust.

Spiritual power is unleashed through the practice of "offering up" sacrifices so that the Lord's plans may be fulfilled: "By offerings and sacrifices to Jesus, everything will be fulfilled that is planned" (January 9, 1986).

Lent, 1986, brought a request for all "little sacrifices" to be offered to God, and speaks of spiritual reward for such sacrifices:

> Dear children, today I am calling you to live this Lent with your little sacrifices. Thank you for every sacrifice you have brought me. Dear children, live in such a way continuously and with love. Help me to bring offerings of your sacrifices to God for which He will reward you.

Finally, the message for Holy Thursday, March 27, 1986, expresses the purpose of this practice:

> Dear children, I wish to thank you for your sacrifices and I invite you to the greatest sacrifice, the sacrifice of love.

> Without love you are not able to accept either me or my Son. Without love you cannot witness your experience to others. That is why I invite you, dear children, to begin to live the love in your hearts.

Lumen Gentium strongly endorses the offerings of one's daily trials and sufferings in the chapter on the Laity.

The daily events of the Christian life, and in particular, trials patiently endured "in the Spirit," are offerings pleasing to the Father:

> For all their works, prayer, and apostolic undertakings, family and married life, daily work, relaxation of mind and body, if they are accomplished in the Spirit — indeed even the hardships of life if patiently borne — all these become spiritual sacrifices acceptable to God through Jesus Christ" (cf. Pet 2:5) (L.G., No. 34).

This offering is given to the Father most appropriately during the Eucharist: "In celebration of the Eucharist these (sacrifices) may most fittingly be offered to the Father along with the Body of the Lord" (L.G., No. 34).

Salvific Doloris (On the Christian Meaning of Human Suffering) also specifically refers to the practice of offering one's suffering to God. In it Pope John Paul II states that this practice is effective in bringing about unity among all mankind:

> And so there should come together in spirit beneath the Cross on Calvary all suffering people who believe in Christ, and particularly those who suffer because of their faith in Him who is the Crucified and Risen One, so that the offering of their sufferings may hasten the fulfillment of the prayer of the Saviour Himself that all may be one (S.D., No. 31).

Lastly, John Paul II points to Our Lady as the greatest example of one who shared in the sufferings of Christ and was united with the Passion of Christ with all her being:

> …It was on Calvary that Mary's suffering, beside the suffering of Jesus, reached an intensity which can hardly be imagined from a human point of view…As a witness to her Son's Passion by her presence, as a sharer in it by her compassion, Mary offered a unique contribution to the Gospel of suffering…She truly has a

special title to be able to claim that she "completes in her flesh" — as already in her heart — "what is lacking in Christ's afflictions" (S.D., No. 25).

Abandon Yourselves Totally

Abandonment to God does not mean to withdraw all human effort for the day-to-day living of the Christian life and expect God to accomplish everything. Abandonment is an unfailing trust and reliance on the workings of God in the daily events of life. This is a perfection of Christian hope and involves either an active or passive response of loving obedience to the will of God depending on the situation. It is best exemplified in Mary's fiat, "Let it be done unto me . . ." spoken at the Annunciation.

Abandonment to God is another strong theme in the message of Medjugorje. Jelena reported this message on June 16, 1983:

> Abandon yourselves totally to God. Renounce disordered passions. Reject fear and give yourself; those who know how to abandon themselves will no longer know either fear or obstacles.

The Gospel passage read every Thursday (Matthew 6:24-34) by members of the parish is a profound call to a deeper trust and faith in the Heavenly Father. It is a call to "seek first of all His kingdom and His righteousness and all these things shall be yours."

Abandonment to God is particularly effective in the battle against Satan:

> Dear children, pray, because Satan is continually trying to thwart my plans. Pray with your hearts and in prayer **give yourselves up to Jesus** (August 11, 1984).

Complete surrender to God enables one to live the message of Medjugorje completely:

> Dear children, I invite you to decide completely for God. I beg you, dear children, to surrender yourselves completely and you will be able to live everything I say to you. It will not be difficult for you to surrender yourselves completely to God (January 2, 1986).

Abandonment to the Holy Spirit allows Jesus to strengthen the believer and work through the individual:

> Open your hearts to the Holy Spirit in a special way these days. The Holy Spirit

is working in a special way through you.
Open your hearts and give your life to
Jesus so that He may work through your
hearts and strengthen you" (May 23,
1985).

Our Lady has frequently asked for an
abandonment to herself as a sure means of complete
abandonment to God: "Consecrate yourselves to the
Immaculate Heart. Abandon yourselves totally. I will
protect you" (August 2, 1983).

Abandonment to Our Lady as loving mother will
result in her guidance:

Dear children, abandon yourselves to me
so that I can lead you totally. Do not be
preoccupied with the material things of
this world (April 24, 1986).

The conciliar and post-conciliar documents of
the Church speak of this same type of abandonment to
God. **Dei Verbum** (Constitution on Divine Revelation)
highlights man's freedom to surrender himself in faith
to God: "By faith man freely commits his entire self to
God, making 'the full submission of his intellect and will
to God . . .'" (D.V. No. 5).

Abandonment to the Holy Spirit is acknowledged
in Paul VI's document, **Evangelii Nuntiandi**. This is
found as well in the message of Medjugorje:

The faithful are striving everywhere, not merely to know and understand Him [the Holy Spirit] better . . . but also to surrender themselves to Him with joyous hearts, opening their minds to His inspiration. They are eager to be guided by Him (E.N., No. 75).

The same post-conciliar document associates abandonment to God with obedience to His will:

Men and women are called to obey the will of God freely in all things. This is "the obedience of faith by which people freely commit their entire selves to God" (D.V., No. 5) (G.C.D., No. 64).

It is evident, then that the various devotional calls of the Medjugorje message have their parallels in the mind of the official teaching authority of the Church. To participate in the sacramental and spiritual life of the Body of Christ is to say "yes" both to Vatican II's universal call to Christian holiness and to the spiritual directives of the message of Medjugorje.

Chapter V

Lourdes and Fatima

In 1858 in a grotto outside of Lourdes, France, the Blessed Mother appeared in a series of eighteen apparitions to Bernadette Soubirous, an illiterate village girl. In 1917 in Fatima, Portugal, three young shepherds reported apparitions of an Angel of Peace and subsequent monthly apparitions of the Virgin Mary. Both Lourdes and Fatima, as well as other lesser known apparitions of Our Lady, after intensive investigation by the Church have been approved for belief and devotion by the faithful.[1]

How does the urgent call to humanity given by the "Queen of Peace" compare with the messages given by the "Immaculate Conception" and "Our Lady of the Rosary?" Are there common themes, elements or patters of development that can be discerned between the three sets of apparitions? Does the message of the "Gospa," as the young visionaries refer to her, coincide with those of Fatima and Lourdes? Has the message Our Lady proclaims developed from one set of apparitions to another? These questions will help us identify the authenticity of Medjugorje.

The Message of Lourdes

Fourteen-year-old Bernadette Soubirous was gathering firewood on the afternoon of February 11, 1858, when she saw a beautiful, young lady standing in a grotto across the river Gave. She described the "lady" she saw at Massabielle as "dressed in white with a blue sash, yellow roses, the color of the chain of her rosary, on each foot."

During the second apparition Bernadette sprinkled holy water upon the "lady" to which she smiled in return. (This same incident was reported by Vicka during the third Medjugorjian apparition.) Bernadette was asked by the Lady to return to the grotto for fourteen days, and told as well that she would not be happy in this world but in the next.

Some of the remaining apparitions were without any publicly revealed messages but much is known by her testimony and by the reports of onlookers. Bernadette was given three secrets with the directive, "I forbid you to repeat this to anyone." Bernadette was told to "pray for sinners." She turned to the crowd during the eighth apparition and repeated the words of the Lady: "Penitence, penitence, penitence!" During the ninth vision she was told to perform acts of penance, one of which uncovered the miraculous spring at Lourdes. She performed similar penitential acts during the remaining apparitions.

Bernadette's face would undergo an obvious change of countenance at the appearance of the Virgin Mary. Her lips moved but no sound was heard by those around her unless she turned to address the crowd directly. The visionaries in Medjugorje also seem to transcend time and space during the time of the apparitions.

During the seventeenth apparition, the flame from a large candle touched the skin of Bernadette's left hand for fifteen minutes without the least trace of physical harm. Bernadette prayed the rosary before, during, and after most apparitions (as is the Medjugorjian practice).

Though the actual content of the messages at Lourdes is succinct, it is consistent. The fundamental message is the call to prayer and penance offered for the conversion of sinners. This is seen in the many acts of penance Bernadette herself performed, in the few messages she disclosed, and in her frequent recitation of the rosary.

The apparitions were approved as authentic by the Church on January 18, 1862.

Fatima

Three shepherd children were visited by an "Angel of Peace" in 1916 in the fields outside of Fatima, Portugal. The angel told the children on more than one occasion to "Pray, pray very much!" He spoke to them of the hearts of Jesus and Mary and told them to "Make everything you can a sacrifice, and offer it to God...for the conversion of sinners. You will thus draw down peace upon you country.." During the third appearance the angel gave them the Eucharist and told them to receive it in reparation for sinners.

The following May while the three children, Lucia, Jacinta and Francisco, were in the fields tending the sheep and playing a game, the Virgin Mary appeared to them standing above a small holmoak tree. She asked them if they were willing to offer themselves to God and to bear all the suffering that He willed to send them as reparation for the conversion of sinners. During this same vision she told them to "Pray the rosary every day, in order to obtain peace for the world and for the end of the war."

During the second apparition she requested that they return the next month and told Lucia, "My Immaculate Heart will be your refuge and the way that will lead you to God."

The third message on July 13, 1917, introduced the title "Our Lady of the Rosary" and reemphasized the directive to pray the daily rosary with the goal of world peace and the end of World War I. The three visionaries also saw hell and in the midst of the vision Our Lady delivered a message of salvation: devotion to the Immaculate Heart of Mary will save many souls and establish peace. She also prophesied a second world war, famine, persecutions of the Church, and specific sufferings for the Pope. Our Lady asked for the conservation of Russia to her Immaculate Heart and the Communion of Reparation on five consecutive first Saturdays.

During the fourth and fifth apparitions the Virgin Mary promised to perform a miracle "so that all may believe."

During the last three apparitions she also asked that a chapel be built on the spot and repeated her request of the daily rosary. She stressed the need for conversion and repentance, and urged all of humanity to cease offending God. Throughout the apparitions the need for devotion to the Immaculate Heart was stressed. A seventh apparition to Lucia in 1925 underscored the same themes of reparation, devotion, and the rosary, and specified the requested five first Saturdays of Reparation. Our Lady promised the graces of salvation to all who, on the first Saturday of five consecutive months, shall "confess, receive Holy Communion, recite five decades of the rosary, and keep me company for fifteen minutes" while meditating on the rosary, all with the intention of offering reparation to her Immaculate Heart.

The apparitions at Fatima were approved by the Church in 1931.

Fatima: A Development of Lourdes

The message of Fatima is a development of Lourdes. At Lourdes the Blessed Mother directed Bernadette to prayer and penance for the conversion of sinners. The call to pray the rosary was implicitly present. The Fatima messages continued those themes but developed them extensively. The children were directed to "offer up" their sacrifices and sufferings. This also called for the establishment of devotion to the Immaculate Heart of Mary, for the Saturday Communions of Reparation, and for the explicit global call for peace. Let us now examine how the messages of Medjugorje compare as both a continuation and a development of the messages of Lourdes and Fatima.[2]

Medjugorje: A Continuation

It is readily apparent that the theme of the message of Medjugorje coincides with the major elements of the Marian apparitions of Lourdes and Fatima. Since Fatima contains the same elements as Lourdes, we will compare the Fatima message to that of Medjugorje. In that way we will indirectly compare Lourdes to Medjugorje as well.

The overall message of Fatima stresses the necessity of prayer, particularly the rosary, and the offering of self in sufferings and sacrifices to obtain the conversion of sinners and world peace, through devotion to the Immaculate Heart of Mary. The theme of reparation is strongly emphasized, specifically through the Eucharist. These major currents throughout the angelic and Marian apparitions find parallels in Our Lady's message in Medjugorje. Of course, there are different degrees of emphasis just as there are between

Lourdes and Fatima, or between the precious apparitions of Our Lady at Guadalupe, Rue de Bac and so forth.

The call to pray and do penance for the conversion of sinners, for world peace, and for adoration of God is pre-eminent in both Fatima and Medjugorje. The rosary is continually stressed as the most powerful means to achieve these ends.

It is frequent recitation of the rosary that will gain Francisco's immediate entry into heaven. Each of the seven apparitions (including the one in 1925) contained the directive to pray the daily rosary. Above all, it is by the title "Our Lady of the Rosary" that the Blessed Virgin wished to be known at Fatima.

The rosary, as we have seen, is also stressed in Medjugorje. The message given to Jakov to "Let all the prayers which you say in your houses in the evening be said for the conversion of sinners...Pray the rosary every evening" is an example of two themes emphasized at Fatima: conversion of sinners and the rosary. The message is being restated in our day. One of the developments of the message of Fatima is the Medjugorjian call for the daily recitation of the fifteen-decade rosary. Of special note is the request Our Lady has made that priests pray the rosary and "give time to the rosary" (June 25, 1985).

Prayer is meant to obtain the conversion of sinners and world peace both in Fatima and Medjugorje. Both series of apparitions continually stress the need for faith and prayer to obtain healings of body and soul, conversion of sinners, and relief for the souls suffering in purgatory.

The Fatima themes of self-abandonment and offering sufferings and sacrifices to God for the conversion of sinners and in reparation for the offenses against God also are paralleled in Medjugorje. The Madonna has frequently expressed her sorrow and suffering because of the sinfulness of the world and the lack of response to Jesus Christ: "If you only knew what I go through, you would never sin again" (Nov. 6, 1983); or the message from April 26, 1984: "Dear children, sympathize with me. Pray, pray, pray!" This message is very similar to Mary's words during the seventh apparition to Lucia: "Have compassion on the Heart of your most Holy Mother . . ."

The theme of Eucharistic reparation given at Fatima is repeated in the Medjugorjian message by Mary's directive to "make atonement for sins committed against the Sacred Heart" and the summons to daily Mass and adoration of the Blessed Sacrament.

The visionaries of both Fatima and Medjugorje have experienced the reality of hell. In addition, both series of apparitions clearly refer to heaven and purgatory as states of life after death. At both Fatima and Medjugorje, Our Lady predicted world catastrophes in the near future. In both messages there was an element of the conditional: at Fatima Our Lady clearly stated that the war and the calamities could be averted if her message was heeded; at Medjugorje Our Lady has already indicated that at least one of the impending disasters has been averted and others have been mitigated because of prayer and fasting in response to her call.

At Fatima, Mary's visits were preceeded by an angel who declared himself to be "The Angel of Peace"; in our day it is "The Queen of Peace" herself who is appearing.

Medjugorje: New Elements in the Marian Message

There are some new elements in the message of Medjugorje that were not present in the apparitions at Fatima. It is important, however, to realize that these do not change the essential direction of the Marian message begun at Lourdes. The basic difference are simply in the ways the call to faith, prayer, penance, and conversion can be lived out in the life of the believer.

The only new theme not explicitly contained in the message of Fatima is the call to fasting, which is central to the Medjugorjian message. Fasting is a specific form of penance and as such is consistent with the directives of Fatima. It is also worth noting that in 1917 fasting was a normative, obligatory practice of the Church: midnight Eucharistic fasts, meatless Friday fasts, etc. Today fasting in the Church can be substituted for by a variety of other penances, according to Canon Law.

Other new elements of the message of Medjugorje that do not appear in the Fatima message are: renewal in the Holy Spirit, ecumenism, renewal of Sacred Scripture, and the emphasis on family and community prayer. It has been shown that these areas are in conformity with the contemporary teaching of the Magesterium. Therefore, though they do not have explicit parallels in the Fatima message, they find ample parallels in post-conciliar teaching.

Furthermore, each of these areas — a deeper faith and renewal in the Holy Spirit, reading the Bible, increase of family and community prayer, and true ecumenism — are specific ways of living out the message given first at Lourdes, developed at Fatima, and continued at Medjugorje. Therefore, even though they are not explicitly stated, they in no way contradict the Fatima message.

Medjugorje: A Harmonious Call

In summary, it is clear that the message of Medjugorje contains the basic themes of Lourdes and Fatima. All three are repeated summons to prayer and penance in reparation to God for the sins of humanity, in supplication for the conversion of sinners, and for peace for the world. At Medjugorje Our Lady teaches her children how to respond in this day and age in specific, concrete ways to that fundamental call. There are some new elements that are not previously apparent in the apparitions at Fatima or Lourdes, yet they are authentic representations of the post-conciliar direction of the Church.

It is fitting that Our Lady, as a wise mother, would shape her message to respond to the needs and currents of the time. It is also logical that the message given by the Madonna would reflect the current emphases in the Church as guided by the Holy Spirit during the same historical period. An example of this would be the apparitions at Lourdes where Our Lady proclaimed "I am the Immaculate Conception," a dogma which had been solemnly defined only four years earlier by Pope Pius IX.

Medjugorje is a harmonius call bringing together the message of Fatima and Lourdes with the post-conciliar direction of the Magesterium in words and actions particularly suitable for the modern world.

Medjugorje and the Church

The messages of Our Lady from Medjugorje, as reported by the Croatian visionaries, is a Christian message crucial for our present age.

After reading the words of the Madonna and examining them in light of defined sources of Christian truth and faith, we can conclude confidently that whether or not they represent an authentic modern-day appearance of Mary, Mother of God, the Medjugorjian message is firmly based both in the words of Jesus Christ in the Gospel and in the official teachings of the Catholic Church, and is, therefore, sound, orthodox, and Catholic in content.

On this basis, and **on this basis alone**, every Christian is not only free to live the message of Medjugorje, but is in fact **called** to live the Medjugorjian message, which so beautifully expands the salvific and oftentimes challenging call of Christ in the Gospel. The committed Christian (and further, anyone with an "open heart") is invited to incorporate the Medjugorjian call for a greater generosity of prayer, penance and, consequently, peace into his or her daily life.

The question may arise: can the obedient Catholic accept the contents of private revelation and incorporate them into one's life before the Church makes an official pronouncement regarding the apparition? The answer, by the Church's own teaching and experience, is yes — provided that after **prudent** and **cautious** examination of the reported revelation there is nothing found in the contents of the revealed message that in any way is counter to magisterial teachings on faith and morals. It is precisely the contents of any reported apparition that the Church carefully examines and evaluates before she grants official "negative approval." This does not guarantee the authenticity of the respective apparition but merely states that nothing contained in the revealed message is doctrinally against faith and morals, and therefore is in no sense dangerous for the faithful.

The faithful can begin to act upon the contents of private revelation before final ecclesiastical approval is given. If this were not so then the visionaries at Fatima and all those who accepted Mary's message in 1917 would be classified as "disobedient" Catholics, since the apparitions were not given official ecclesiastical approval until 1931, some thirteen years after the events. The Church remains at once cautious and just in her consistently balanced approach to the domain of private revelation. Medjugorje thereby remains open for acceptance and incorporation by any individual as the Church continues her official investigation.

Conclusion: An Open Heart

Medjugorje proclaims a message of true peace, a peace built upon the spiritual peace of Christ, directed to an age seemingly headed for its own moral, spiritual and possibly physical destruction. The message of Medjugorje is unmistakably a Christian message, a Marian message. I would like to conclude by quoting the theologian Garrrigou-La Grange, O.P.[3] There words written in the 1930's are almost a theological prophecy of our present situation, and do well to summarize the heart of the message of Medjugorje's call to peace for the modern world:

> Exterior peace will not be obtained for the world except by the interior peace of souls, bringing them back to God and working to establish the reign of Christ, in the depths of their intellects, of their hearts, and of their wills. For this return

of straying souls to Him who alone can save them, it is necessary to have recourse to the intercession of Mary, universal mediatrix, and Mother of all men. It is said of sinners who seem forever lost that they must be confided to Our Lady; it is the same for Christian peoples who stray. All the influence of the Blessed Virgin has its goal to lead them to her Son . . . This is why on all sides many interior souls, before the unprecedented disorders and tragic sufferings of the hour, feel the need for recourse to the redeeming love of Christ, through the intercession of Mary Mediatrix.

Notes

[1] Private revelation consists of a supernatural manifestation of Christian truth made after the close of public revelation (Sacred Scripture and Tradition) with the death of the last apostle. The Church can give her "negative approval" to a private revelation or apparition by stating that there is nothing contained in it contrary to faith and morals. In approving an apparition or a revelation, the Church does not intend to guarantee the authenticity of the respective private revelation, but states that the content of the apparition can be accepted by the faithful without any doctrinal danger in regard to faith and morals.

It is considered reprehensible for any member of the faithful to contradict or ridicule a revelation after the Church has given her negative approval. Further, if after prudent judgement, it has been personally determined that a given revelation is authentic, the one who has received the revelation should accept it in the spirit of faith, and if the private revelation contains any message for others, those persons also have an obligation to accept the truth of the revelation and act upon it. Cf J. Aumann, O.P., *Spiritual Theology*, London, Sheed and Ward, 1979, p. 429.

[2] For a more comprehensive treatment of the similarities and difference between Fatima and Medjugorje see: *The Message of Medjugorje: The Marian Message to the Modern World*, by the author, University Press of America, 1986.

[3] Reginald Garrigou-La Grange, O.P., *The Mother of the Saviour and our Interior Life*, translated by Bernard Kelly, C.S.S.P., Dublin, Golden Books, Ltd., 1948, p. 317.

Chapter VI

Words of the Queen of Peace

The direct words from the Gospa are here presented in a basic chronological order. Our Lady's words have not been recorded in any comprehensive or methodological manner since the confiscation of the rectory's original records by local police authorities towards the beginning of the apparitions. The messages that appear below have been approved by the parish priests of St. James in Medjugorje as actual messages from the Queen of Peace.

Messages of the First Seven Days
June 24 to June 30, 1981

June 25, 1981: The first words spoken by Our Lady to the youths occurred on the second day of the apparitions when she answered a question about Ivanka's mother who had died two months earlier. Our Lady responded that her mother is "well, is with her," and that Ivanka should not worry. Ivanka then asked whether her mother had any message for her children, to which Our Lady responded, "Obey your grandmother and be good to her, for she is old and cannot work." Mary ended the apparition with the words, "Go in God's peace."

June 26, 1981: On the third day of the apparitions, Vicka began the dialogue by sprinkling holy water upon the apparition and saying, "If you are really Our Lady, then stay with us. If not, leave us." Mary's response was a smile. The children then asked Mary who she was, and why she had come to their village. Mary responded, "I am the Blessed Virgin Mary." She continued, "I am here because there are many good believers here. I want to be with you, and to convert and reconcile all people." The visionaries also reported an apparition later in the day where Mary repeated the parting words, "Go in God's peace."

As one of the visionaries, Marija, was walking home from that evening apparition, she reported a further apparition of Mary, with tears in her eys, positioned in front of a cross without a corpus. Mary spoke the words, "Peace, peace, peace...nothing but peace. Men must be reconciled with God and with one another. For this to happen, it is necessary to believe, to pray, to fast, and to go to Confession. Go in God's peace."

June 27, 1981: The fourth day of the apparition brought questions from the children and answers from Our Lady.

Father Jozo Zovko, O.F.M., at the time the pastor of St. James parish at Medjugorje, instructed the children to ask Our Lady whether she had any specific messages for priests. Our Lady responded, "Let the priests firmly believe."

Vicka asked Our Lady to prove to the other people present at the site of the apparition that she was truly present. Our Lady stated, "Let those who do not see believe as if they see."

Mirjana was troubled over the accusations from other local people that the youths were drug addicts or epileptics. Mary's response was, "There has always been injustice in the world, and there always will be. Disregard it."

Ivanka then asked Our Lady her name. Again Mary answered, "I am the Blessed Virgin Mary." Upon leaving, Our Lady said, "Go in God's peace."

Later during that same day, Our Lady said to the youths, "You are my angels, my dear angels…Go in God's peace."

June 28, 1981: On day five of the apparitions, the visionaries and Our Lady had another dialogue of considerable length.

> *Visionaries:* Dear Madonna! What do you wish from us?

> *Our Lady:* Faith and respect for me.

> *Visionaries:* Dear Madonna! Why don't you appear in the church so that everyone sees you?

Our Lady: Blessed are they who have not seen and have believed.

Visionaries: Dear Madonna! Will you come again?

Our Lady nodded, but did not reply.

Visionaries: Dear Madonna! Do you prefer us to pray to you or to sing to you?

Our Lady: Do both, sing and pray.

Visionaries: Dear Madonna! What do you wish from these people who have gathered here?

Our Lady: Let them believe as if they had seen.

At this point in the dialogue, Our Lady left. The children thought that Our Lady would return, since she had not said her usual parting words, "Go in God's peace." As the children began praying, Our Lady appeared a second time. The children began to seing a traditional Marian song to her, at which point the dialogue resumed.

Our Lady: My angels, my dear angels.

Visionaries: Dear Madonna! What do you wish from these people here?

Our Lady: Let these people who do not see me believe in the same way as the six of you who see me.

Visionaries: Dear Madonna! Shall you leave us some sign here on the earth so that we may convince these people that we are not liars, that we do not lie, that we are not merely playing around with you?

Our Lady: Go in God's peace.

The children also asked Our Lady on this day how she would like them to pray. Our Lady responded, "Continue to recite seven times the Our Father, Hail Mary, Glory Be, and the Creed."

June 29, 1981: On the sixth day, the youths had the following conversation with Our Lady and requested the healing of three-year old Danijel Setka, who was unable to speak due to infant paralysis.

Visionaries: Dear Madonna! Are you glad that the people are here? (Our Lady smiled in confirmation.)

Visionaries: Dear Madonna! How many days are you going to stay with us?

Our Lady: As long as you wish.

Visionaries: Dear Madonna! Are you going to leave us any sign?

Our Lady: I am going to come again tomorrow.

Visionaries: Dear Madonna! What do you wish from these people?

Our Lady: There is only one God and one faith. Believe firmly.

Visionaries: Are we going to be able to endure this? Many are persecuting us because we see.

Our Lady: You will, my angels.

Visionaries: Dear Madonna! What wish do you have for us here?

Our Lady: That you have firm faith and confidence.

Visionaries: Dear Madonna! Can this lady (Dr. Darinka Glamuzina sent from Citluk to investigate) touch you?

Our Lady: There have always been unfaithful Judases. Let her come.

Visionaries: (to the crowd) She is touching her...She left! She left! (The children resume singing with the crowd and Our Lady returns.)
     Light! Light! Here she is! Here she is!

Visionaries: Dear Madonna. Will this little boy Danijel ever be able to speak? Do a miracle so that all will believe us. Dear Madonna. Do a miracle...Dear Madonna. Say something. Dear Madonna. Say something, we ask you. Say something dear Madonna!

Our Lady: Let them (Danijel's parents) firmly believe that he will be healed. Go in God's peace.[1]

June 30, 1981: On the seventh day of the apparitions, Father Jozo Zovko, O.F.M., the parish pastor at the time, interviewed the visionaries immediately after the apparition. The youths had the following message.

> *Father Jozo:* Mirjana, what did you talk about with the Madonna?
>
> *Mirjana:* I asked her if she minds that we went from the hill and came to the other place (in the church). She said that she does not mind.
>
> *Ivanka:* We asked if she is going to leave us some sign. She simply and slowly left and again the light was on the hill where the people were.
>
> *Mirjana:* And she said, "Go in God's peace."
>
> *Jakov:* She also said, "my angels" when we asked if she is going to mind appearing to us in the church. She said, "I will not, my angels."

Messages from July 1981 to December 1983

The following messages are those that possess some chronological data, and they will be followed by others given within the general time frame of July 1981 to December 1983.

August 6, 1981: Numerous witnesses, both pilgrims and townspeople, state that the word "MIR" (Croatian for "PEACE") was written in the sky above the hill.

August 7, 1981: The youths reported that Our Lady had asked them to go to the top of the mountain of the cross (a neighboring mountain where in 1933 the townspeople had built a large, concrete cross commemorating the 1900th anniversary of the crucifixion of Christ) at approximately two o'clock in the morning to pray that the people would do penance for sinners. She then promised to give a special sign so that the world would believe.

August 1981: The youths asked Our Lady what was the "best fast." Our Lady answered, "A fast of bread and water."

End of August 1981: Our Lady conveyed these words concerning her title, "I am the Queen of Peace."

September 4, 1981: Our Lady said the sign for unbelievers would be given after the apparitions ended.

October 1981: Ivica Vego, a priest from Mostar, requested the visionaries to ask Our Lady the following three questions.

What will happen in and to Poland? Mary replied, "There will soon be great conflicts there, but in the end the righteous will triumph."

Will the "case of Hercegovinga" be resolved satisfactorily (a reference to the controversy between the Franciscan Order and the Episcopal authority in Hercegovina)? Our Lady responded, "The problem will be resolved satisfactorily. There is need of prayer and penance."

The third question pertained to the world conflict between the East and West, to which Our Lady answered, "Russia is the people where God will be most glorified. The West has advanced in civilization but without God as though it were it own creator." Mary's message continued; but Mirjana, the visionary who voiced the questions and received the answers was unable to disclose the rest, as it would have disclosed an aspect of the secrets.

October 22, 1981: Many people reported seeing the large concrete cross on the top of the mountain turn to a pillar of light with the figure of a woman, as a statue, at the foot of the cross. This continued for approximately thirty minutes, and was preceded by the following message from Our Lady, "All these signs are to reinforce your faith until I send the permanent, visible sign."

December 7, 1981: "Many people are on the way to conversion, but not all."

December 8, 1981: (Feast of the Immaculate Conception) The visionaries saw Our Lady on her knees, praying these words, "My beloved Son. Please forgive these numerous sins with which humanity is offending

You." After praying with the children, Our Lady told them that she prays daily at the foot of the cross, asking her Son to forgive the sins of humanity.

January 1982: At the beginning of the month, Our Lady was again seen by several pilgrims and priests in a position of prayer at the foot of the cross. Father Tomislav Vlasic, spiritual director of the visionaries at the time, requested the youths to ask Our Lady whether it was in fact she at the foot of the cross on the mountain. The answer given was, "It is understandable that I am praying at the foot of the cross. The cross is a sign of salvation. My Son suffered on the cross; He redeemed the world on the cross. Salvation comes from the cross."

July 21, 1982: "Christians have forgotten that they can prevent war and even natural calamities by prayer and fasting."

August 6, 1982: Our Lady requested monthly Confession, which was immediately implemented by the parish.

August 1982: Ivan, one of the visionaries, was on the hillside with friends when Our Lady appeared to him and spoke the following words, "Now I will give you a sign to strengthen your faith." Ivan reported two bright beams of light coming down, one that rested upon the church, and another upon the cross on the mountain. The same phenomenon was reported by Ivan's friends.

Spring 1983: "Hasten your conversion. Do not wait for the sign that has been announced for the unbelievers; it will already be too late for them to have a conversion. You who believe, be converted, and deepen your faith.

April 20, 1983: The only word I wish to speak of is the conversion of the whole world. I wish to speak it to you so that you can speak it to the whole world. I ask nothing but conversion…It is my desire…be converted… leave everything; that comes from conversion. Good-bye now, and may peace be with you."

Messages Given Between July 1981 to December 1983

The visionaries report that Mary's opening greeting is most always, "Praised be Jesus." The visionaries respond by the phrase, "May Jesus and Mary always be praised." Mary's typical closing words are, "Go in God's peace."

Our Lady was asked if there was a need for a parish prayer group. She responded, "Yes, there is a need for a prayer group not only in the parish, but in all parishes. Spiritual renewal is needed for the entire Church."

The pilgrims have frequently asked the Madonna for healings. She replied, "I myself cannot heal you. Only God Himself can heal you. Pray; I will pray with you. Firmly believe, fast, and do penance. I will help you as much as it is in my power. God is helping everybody; I am not God. I need your prayers and sacrifices to help me."

The children reported a complaint from Our Lady because so many believers never pray. She asked the children to call the people to prayer, stating, "Faith cannot be alive without prayer."

On another occasion, Our Lady stated that the best prayer was the Creed. When asked about the Mass, Our Lady responded, "The Mass is the greatest prayer from God, and you will never understand the greatness of it. Therefore, you must be perfect and humble at Mass, and you must be prepared for it."

The visionaries asked whether people should be praying to Jesus or to her. The answer, "Please pray to Jesus. I am His Mother and I intercede for you to Him. But all prayers go to Jesus. I will help, I will pray, but everything does not depend on me, but also on your strength — the strength of those who pray." [2]

The children further reported that Our Lady has shown them heaven, hell, and purgatory (though not all the children saw purgatory and hell, at their own request). While showing them purgatory, Our Lady stated, "Those people are waiting for your prayers and sacrifices." When some of the children were shown hell, Our Lady told them: "This is the punishment for those who do not love God; and many who are alive today will go to hell."

Our Lady frequently requested that the rosary be prayed and has emphasized that every prayer is pleasing to God. Further, she insists that the apparitions should not conflict with the parish Mass times.

During this time Our Lady complained that the practice of fasting in the Church has almost disappeared. She asked believers to fast on Fridays. Fasting and prayer are constantly emphasized as the most powerful means to conversion. She has stated that the giving of alms by the healthy does not constitute a legitimate substitution for fasting. Those who are too ill to fast for themselves can choose some other form of sacrifice, together with the reception of the sacraments of Confession and Holy Communion. Our Lady recommended that people unite in prayer for the seriously ill and for those in serious sin.

The visionaries have reported that many miracles will accompany the arrival of the sign. Our Lady said during this time period, "I know many will not believe you and many enthusiastic for the faith will grow cold. You should stay steadfast and urge the people to steadfast prayer, penance, and conversion. In the end, you will be the happiest."

The visionaries reported this message regarding the diversity of religions:

> In God's eyes there are no divisions. You in the world have made the divisions. The one mediator is Jesus Christ. Which religion you belong to cannot be a matter of indifference. The presence of the Holy Spirit is not the same in every church.

Our Lady has described the Sacrament of Penance as "…a medicine for the Church in the West…Whole regions of the Church would be healed if believers would go to Confession once a month."

On several occasions, the children have reported Our Lady appearing with Christ, either as a child or in His Passion, with the following words, "Do whatever He tells you."

In November of 1983, according to the visionary Marija Pavlovic, Our Lady requested that the Pope and the local bishop be told of the urgency and importance of her messages. Accordingly, Father Vlasic, in conjunction with the visionaries, sent a report to Pope John Paul II.

Messages Reported Between
June 1984 and January 1985

The following messages occurred approximately between June 1984 and January 1985:

Dear children, if you only knew how great my love is for you, you would cry for joy.

Dear children, when someone is standing before you asking a favor of you, respond by giving. I stand before many hearts and they do not open to me. Pray that the world may receive my love.

Dear children, I love you so much, and when you love me, you can feel it. I bless you in the name of the Holy Trinity and in my name. Stay in peace.

Dear children, the love of God has not flowed over the whole world. Pray, therefore.

Dear children, I desire the whole world to become my children, but they are not willing. I want to give them everything. Pray, therefore.

Mirjana received the tenth secret on December 25, 1982. Since then she no longer has regular apparitions of the Blessed Virgin. On that occasion, however, Mirjana was promised an annual "birthday apparition" by Our Lady. The following is Mirjana's account of her 1985 birthday apparition:

There were a number of people there. We started waiting for her at four o'clock in the afternoon. We were praying for fifteen minutes, and then she spent fifteen minutes with us. She greeted me like always, "Praised be Jesus", and I responded. She congratulated me on my birthday and then we started our conversation. First she complained because of unbelievers. She said this, "They are my children and I am suffering because of them, because they do not know what is waiting for them if they do not convert to God. Therefore, Mirjana, pray for them."

Then all of us together prayed. She started two Our Fathers and two Glory Bes for unbelievers. Then she complained about the greed in the world and in Medjugorje as well. She said, "Woe to those who would take everything from those who are coming (to honour her), and blessed are those from whom they are taking." Then we all prayed two Our Fathers and two Glory Be's.

I asked her if all of us could pray for her the Hail Mary, and she smiled at that.

Then we talked about the secrets. I told her that I have many questions (around thirty) for her. She smiled and said to me not to worry about those, because when I come to ask them I will know all the answers, and she will give me that grace. Otherwise, that would take us too much time.

Then I prayed the Hail Holy Queen.

Oh, I forgot something. She was blessing all the holy objects, and when she blessed them I put all next to me. She asked me to give her the rosary. Then she took it and started praying on it and she said, "It is this way to pray on it, tell that to everyone!" She said that the rosary is not supposed to stay as a decoration, something many have it for. On March 19, she appeared also. The vision lasted seven minutes. There were four of us. We talked about the secrets and we prayed. Nothing else important happened. On both days she blessed us.

On May 6, 1985, Ivanka received an apparition that lasted six minutes longer than that of the other visionaries. During this time Our Lady revealed the tenth secret to her. Our Lady then asked Ivanka to wait for her alone on the following day. On May 7, Ivanka reported an apparition at her home that lasted approximately one hour. She no longer sees Our Lady daily. The following is Ivanka's account of this last apparition:

As on every day Our Lady came with the greeting, "Praised be Jesus Christ." I responded, "May Jesus and Mary always be praised."

I never saw Mary so beautiful as this evening. She was so beautiful and gentle. Today she wore the most beautiful gown I had ever seen in my life. Her gown and also her veil and crown had gold and silver sequins of lights. There were two angels with her. They had the same clothes as Our Lady. The angels were beautiful. I don't have the words to describe it. One can only experience it.

Our Lady asked me what I would like. Then I asked to see my earthly mother. Our Lady smiled and nodded her head, and at once my mother appeared. She was smiling. Our Lady told me to stand up. I stood up, my mother embraced me and kissed me and she said, "My child, I am so proud of you." She kissed me and disappeared. After that Our Lady said to me, "My dear child, today is our last meeting. Do not be sad because I will be coming to you on every anniversary (June 25) except this year. Dear child, do not think that you have done anything wrong, or that this is the reason I will not be coming to you. No, you did not. With all your heart you have accepted the plan which my Son and I had, and you have done everything. No one on this earth has had the grace which you and your brothers and sisters had. Be happy because I am your Mother who loves you with my whole heart.

Ivanka! Thank you for responding to the call of my Son, and for persevering and for always remaining with Him as long as He asked you. Dear child, tell all your friends that my Son and myself are always with them when they ask us and call us. What I have spoken to you these years about the secrets, speak to no one until I tell you.

After this I asked Our Lady if I could kiss her. She nodded her head, and I kissed her. I asked her to bless me; she blessed me, smiled, and said, "Go in God's peace," and she departed slowly with the two angels.

Messages Through Jelena Vasilj "The Seventh Visionary"

Jelena Vasilj began reporting locutions and messages from the Blessed Virgin Mary on December 15, 1982. As previously mentioned, Jelena sees and hears Our Lady "with the heart." The Madonna gives Jelena messages that broaden the general messages given to the other six visionaries.

June 16, 1983: I have come to tell the world: God is Truth, He exists. In Him is true happiness and abundance of life. I present myself here as Queen of Peace to tell the world that peace is necessary for the salvation of the world. In God is found true joy from which true peace flows.

Abandon yourself totally to God. Renounce disordered passions. Reject fear and give yourself — those who know how to abandon themselves will no longer know either obstacles or fear.

June 26, 1983: Love your enemies. Pray for them and bless them.

June 28, 1983: *This message was directed to the parish youth group.* Pray at least half an hour morning and evening. Consecrate five minutes to the Sacred Heart; every family is its image.

July 4, 1983: *Again to the youth prayer group.* You have begun to pray three hours, but you look at your watches, preoccupied with your work. Be preoccupied with the one thing necessary, and let yourselves be guided by the Holy Spirit. Then your work will go well. Do not rush. Let your work be guided and you will see that everything will be accomplished well.

Early July 1983: Be alert. This is a dangerous time for you. The devil will try to turn you from this way. Those who give themselves to God will be the object of the attack.

August 2, 1983: Consecrate yourselves to the Immaculate Heart. Abandon yourselves totally. I will protect you. I will pray to the Holy Spirit. Pray to Him yourselves.

August 15, 1983: *(Feast of the Assumption)* Satan is enraged because of those who fast and are converted.

August 25, 1983: Do not be preoccupied. May peace reunite your heart. The trouble comes only from Satan.

September 1983: *These words were addressed to those of the prayer group returning to secular schools and environments.* Be alert not to diminish the spirit of prayer.

October 20, 1983: *A new youth prayer group was to be formed. Our Lady asked for a four-year commitment from them followed by these words:* This is not yet the moment to choose your vocation. The important thing is to first enter into prayer. Afterwards, you will make the right choice.

All families should consecrate themselves to the Sacred Heart every day. I would be very happy if the whole family were to come together for prayer every morning for half an hour.

October 21, 1983: The important thing is to pray to the Holy Spirit that He may descend. When you have Him, you have everything. People make a mistake when they turn only to the saints to ask for something.

October 24, 1983: *A message for the prayer group.* If you pray, a spring of life will flow from your hearts.

October 25, 1983: Pray, pray, pray! Prayer will give you everything. It is through prayer that you can obtain everything.

October 27, 1983: Pray, pray, pray! You will never get anything from debate, but only from prayer. If you are questioned about me and about what I say, answer, "Explanation is useless. It is by praying that we understand best."

October 29, 1983: I see that you are all tired. I want to take you all into my arms so that you can be with me.

October 29, 1983: Prayer is the only way that leads to peace. If you pray and fast, you will obtain all you ask.

October 30, 1983: Why do you not give yourselves completely to me? I know that you pray a long time, but really hand yourselves over. Pray also in the evening when you have finished your day. Sit down in your room and say to Jesus, "Thank you." If in the evening you fall asleep in peace, praying, in the morning you will wake up thinking of Jesus and you will be able to ask Him for peace. But if you fall asleep distracted, in the morning you will be hazy and you will forget even to pray.

November 5, 1983: Be patient; be steadfast; keep praying.

November 8, 1983: Consider how sinful the world is today...It appears to you not to sin because you are here in a peaceful world where there isn't disorder.

But how many have tepid faith, and so do not listen to Jesus. If only you knew what I go through, you would never sin again. I need your prayers. Pray.

November 9, 1983: Don't go to Confession from habit to stay the same after it. No, that is not good. Confession should give drive to your faith. It should stir you, and draw you near to Jesus. If Confession doesn't mean much to you, you will be converted only with difficulty.

November 17, 1983: Pray. Don't look for a reason why I am constantly asking you to pray. Intensify (deepen) your personal prayer and let it spill over to others.

November 18, 1983: In Medjugorje many people are intent on materialism from which they draw some profit, but they forget the one only good.

November 29, 1983: I am your good Mother, and Jesus is your great friend. Fear nothing in His presence, but give Him your hearts. From the depth of your heart tell Him your sufferings. In this way you will be revitalized in prayer, your heart set free, and in peace, without fear.

December 4, 1983: Pray. Pray. If you pray, I shall watch over you and be with you. Pray.

December 29, 1983: I want a great peace, a great love, to grow in you. Pray.

Early January 1984: Our Lady requested through Jelena that the parishioners come to church once during the week so that Our Lady could direct the spiritual life of the parish by way of weekly messages. Thursday was chosen by the parish priests. Since the first Thursday in March 1984, the six visionaries have reported specific messages for the parish during the Thursday evening apparitions. These Thursday Messages will be presented in the following section.

January 8, 1984: Children, pray. I repeat: Pray. I say it to you again. Don't think that Jesus is going to show Himself once again in the crib; but He is being reborn in your hearts.

January 18, 1984: Pray. I wish to carve in each heart the sign of love. If you love every person, there is peace in you. If you are at peace with everyone, peace reigns.

January 27, 1984: Pray and fast. I want you to draw your life from prayer…including each morning on waking, at least five Paters, Aves, Glorias, and a sixth for our Holy Father the Pope. Then the Creed and the prayer to the Holy Spirit. And, if it is possible, it would be good to say the rosary.

February 13, 1984: Fast and pray. Give me your hearts. I want to change them completely. I want to refashion them. I want them to be pure.

February 15, 1984: *These words were received during a cold front with a chilling wind that prevented many people from attending evening Mass.* The wind is my symbol. I shall come in the wind. If the wind blows, know that I am with you. You have learned that the cross represents

Christ. The cross which you have in your homes is a symbol of Him. My symbol is different.

March 1, 1984: *The Virgin Mary requested that the following Gospel passage be read each Thursday.*

> No one can serve two masters; for either he will hate the one and love the other, or he will be devoted to the one and despise the other. You cannot serve God and mammon.
>
> Therefore, I tell you, do not be anxious about your life, what you should eat or what you shall drink, nor want about your body, what you shall put on. Is not life more than food, and the body more than clothing? Look at the birds of the air; they neither sow nor reap nor gather into barns, and yet your Heavenly Father feeds them, Are you not of more value than they? And which of you by being anxious can add one cubit to his span of life? And why are you anxious about your clothing? Consider the lilies in the field, how they grow; they neither toil nor spin; yet I tell you, even Solomon in all his glory was not arrayed like one of these. But if God so clothes the grass of the field, which today is alive and tomorrow is thrown into the oven, will

He not much more clothe you, O men of little faith?

Therefore, do not be anxious, saying, "What shall we eat?" or "What shall we drink"? or "What shall we wear?", for the Gentiles seek all these things; and your Heavenly Father knows that you need them all. But seek first His Kingdom and His righteousness, and all these things shall be yours as well. Therefore, do not be anxious about tomorrow, for tomorrow will be anxious for itself. Let the day's own troubles be sufficient for the day (Mt. 6:24–34).

Also on March 1: Let each one find his or her own way of fasting. The one who smokes should give up smoking, the one who drinks alcohol should not drink it; let each one give up some pleasure. Have these recommendations passed on to the parish.

March 5, 1984: Pray and fast. Ask the Holy Spirit to renew your souls, to renew the whole world.

March 14, 1984: *This message is one of the few public messages given through Mirjana Vasilj, whose messages, also received through inner locutions, are usually only for her own spiritual direction.* Pray and fast so that during the novena, God will overwhelm you with His power.

March 22, 1984: *This message refers to the achievement of an undisclosed aspect of Mary's plans.* Yesterday evening, I told you that one of the first wishes of my plan had been realized.

March 27, 1984: Children, I want the Holy Mass to be the gift of the day for you. Go to it; long for it to begin, because Jesus Himself gives Himself to you during the Mass. So, live for this moment when you are purified. Pray much that the Holy Spirit will renew your parish. If the people assist at Mass in a half-hearted fashion, they return home with cold, empty hearts.

April 8, 1984: I ask you to pray for the conversion of all. For this, I need prayer.

April 15 – April 22, 1984: (*Holy Week*) Raise your hands and open your hearts. Now, in the moment of the Resurrection, Jesus wants to give you a particular gift. This gift of my Son is my gift; it is this: you will undergo trials with great ease. We will be ready and will show you the way out if you will accept us. Do not say that the Holy Year is now over and there is no more need to pray. On the contrary, reinforce your prayers, because the Holy Year is just one step forward.[3]

After receiving these words, Jelena reported a vision of the risen Jesus. As light radiated from His wound onto the people, Jelena said the risen Jesus spoke these words, Receive My graces and tell the whole world there will be happiness only through Me.

April 19, 1984: (*Holy Thursday*) I will tell you a spiritual secret: If you want to be stronger than evil, make an active conscience for yourself — that is, pray a reasonable amount in the morning; read a text of Holy

Scripture and plant the divine word in your heart; and try to live it during the day, especially in moments of trial — so you will be stronger than evil.

May 23, 1984: *Through Jelena, Our Lady expressed the desire for the parish to have a novena in preparation for the reception of the Sacrament of Confirmation on the Feast of the Ascension, May 31, 1984.*

June 2, 1984: *Through Jelena, Our Lady requested another novena in preparation for the Feast of Pentecost, June 10, 1984.*

Mid–June 1984: *Jelena reported that Our Lady asked for a preparation in prayer for the third anniversary of the beginning of the apparitions, and that June 25 be annually celebrated as the "Feast of Mary, Queen of Peace."*

August 1984: *At the beginning of the month, Jelena transmitted a message intended for "the Pope and all Christians" that established the exact date of Mary's birthday as August 5. Her message requested a preparation for her two-thousandth-year birthday, August 5, 1984.* Throughout the centuries I have dedicated my entire life to you. Is it too much for you to dedicate three days for me? Do not do any work on that day (her birthday) but take your rosaries in your hands and pray. *Our Lady specified fasting and prayer as the means of preparation for the feast of her birthday, and she predicted "great conversions" on that day.*

The following messages reported by Jelena are without specific chronological data but fall into the general time between **December 15, 1982** *and* **November 1984**.

Concerning prayer in the family, Our Lady stated, "I know that every family can pray four hours a day." Jelena responded: "But if I tell this to people, they may back out." Our Lady replied, "Even you do not understand. It is only one-sixth of the day." Jelena confirmed, "I know that you want us to pray continuously."

Regarding the increased quality of prayer, Our Lady stated, "When I say, 'Pray, pray, pray,' I do not mean only increase the hours of prayer, but increase the desire to pray and to be in contact with God; to be in a continuous prayerful state of mind."

Our Lady has indicated to Jelena that peace is needed for prayer. Peace should be present before prayer and during prayer, and that prayer should indeed conclude with peace and reflection.

At one point, before it was publicly known, Jelena began reading a book discussing the possible contents of the third secret from the Fatima apparitions in 1917, and became anxious and afraid over the thought of world punishments and wars. When Our Lady spoke to her later that day, her message was, "Do not think about wars, chastisements, evil. It is when you concentrate on these things that you are on the way to enter into them. Your responsibility is to accept divine peace, to live it."

"If you want to be very happy, live a simple life, be humble, pray much, and do not worry about your problems; let them be settled by God."

In response to the numerous questions presented by the visionaries, Our Lady has responded to Jelena on several occasions, "Why so many questions? The answer is in the Gospel."

Concerning the unavoidability of upcoming catastrophes, Jelena has conveyed these words of Our Lady: "This comes from false prophets. They say, 'On such a day at such a time there will be a catastrophe.' I have always said, 'The evil (the punishment) will come if the world is not converted!' Call people to conversion. Everything depends on your conversion."

At Jelena's request to know the secrets revealed to the other six visionaries, Our Lady responded, "Excuse me. That gift is for the others; it is not yours. What the six young people have said will happen. It is for you to believe like the rest."

Our Lady has said to Jelena when she has experienced difficulties, "Do not defend yourself, but rather pray."

Finally, "I wish you to be a flower which will bloom for Jesus at Christmas — a flower which will not cease blooming when Christmas is over. I wish your hearts to be shepherds for Jesus."

Up to March, 1985, Jelena received messages from Our Lady solely by means of inner locutions, as was also the case with Mirjana Vasilj, her young prayer partner. As of April, 1985, both Jelena and Mirjana have begun to receive visions of Our Lady, in some sense similar to but different from the three-dimensional manner of the apparitions the other visionaries have of the Blessed Virgin. The following is a message transmitted by Jelena in April 1985, at the beginning of the visions:

Jelena: You are beautiful.

Our Lady: I am beautiful because I love. If you want to become beautiful, love!

Notes

1   The parents of Danijel Setka reported the cure of their son at the beginning of November, 1981.

2   "All prayers go to Jesus" seems to point more to the ultimate recipient of prayer, namely Christ, by way of Mary's role as intercessor, than to any prohibition of prayer said directly to Mary. The call to consecrate oneself to the Immaculate Heart of Mary would support this conclusion.

3   1983–84 Holy Year of Redemption.

Chapter VII

Thursday and Monthly Messages

Thursday Messages

As previously mentioned, Jelena reported Our Lady's desire to have the parish dedicate one day a week for spiritual and pastoral direction. The parish priests decided that Thursday would be set aside for this purpose. The six visionaries (usually through Marija) began receiving these special messages in March 1984. These continued until January 8, 1987, when the Madonna revealed the last Thursday Message and began giving one message a month, on the 25th of every month. We here provide a complete listing of the Thursday Messages to date. They make up a profound spiritual and pastoral series of counsels intended to lead the parish community on the path to Christian holiness.

March 1, 1984: Dear children, I have chosen this parish in a special way and I wish to lead it. I am watching over the parish with love and I wish them all to be mine. Thank you for your response this evening. I wish all of you always to be in great numbers with me and my Son. Every Thursday I will say a special message for you.

March 8, 1984: Dear children, convert. In this parish, start converting yourselves. In that way all those who come here will be able to convert.

March 15,1984: This evening, dear children, I am grateful to you in a special way for being here. Unceasingly adore the Most Blessed Sacrament of the Altar. I am always present when the faithful are adoring. Special graces are then being received.

March 22, 1984: Dear children, this evening I am asking you in a special way during Lent to honor the wounds of my Son, which He received from the sins of this parish. Unite with my prayers for this parish so that His sufferings may become bearable.[1] Dear children, endeavor to come in greater numbers.

March 29, 1984: Dear children, this evening in a special way I am asking for your perseverance in trials. Ponder how the Almighty is still suffering today because of your sins. So when the sufferings come, offer them as your sacrifice to God. Thank you for having responded to my call.

April 5, 1984: Dear children, This evening I am especially asking you to venerate the Heart of my Son, Jesus. Make an atonement for the wounds inflicted upon the Heart of my Son. That Heart has been offended with all sorts of sins. Thank you for having responded to my call.

April 12, 1984: Dear children, this evening I ask you to stop slandering and pray for the unity of the parish. For my Son and I have a special plan for this parish. Thank you for having responded to my call.

April 19, 1984: Dear children, sympathize with me. Pray, pray, pray!

April 26, 1984: *This Thursday, the visionaries received no message from Our Lady. Marija concluded that Our Lady was only going to give the Thursday Messages through Lent. Four days later, Marija asked Our Lady during the daily apparition the following question: "Dear Madonna, why have you not given me the message to the parish on (last) Thursday?" Our Lady replied:* I do not wish to force anyone to anything he doesn't feel and doesn't wish, even though I had special messages for the parish to awaken the faith of every believer. But only a small number have accepted the messages on Thursdays. At the beginning there were more of them. But now it looks as if it has become something ordinary to them. And now some have been asking recently for the message out of their curiosity and not out of their faith and devotion to my Son and me.

May 10, 1984: *The parish was concerned that Our Lady would no longer give specific Thursday messages for them. However, the following Thursday Our Lady said*: I am still speaking to you and I intend to continue so. Only listen to my instructions.

May 17, 1984: Dear children, today I am very happy because there are many of those who desire to devote themselves to me. I thank you! You have not been mistaken. My Son, Jesus Christ, wishes to bestow on you special graces through me. My Son is happy because of your dedication.

May 24, 1984: Dear children, I have told you already that I have chosen you in a special way, the way you are. I, your Mother, love you all. And in any moment when it is difficult for you, do not be afraid! I love you even then when you are far from me and my Son. I ask you not to allow my heart to cry with blood because of the souls which get lost in sin. Therefore, dear children, pray, pray, pray! Thank you for having responded to my call.

May 31, 1984: *(Feast of the Ascension) There were many pilgrims present at St. James Church, and that evening Our Lady offered no message. But Mirjana reported that Our Lady said she would give the parish a message on Saturday, to be announced on Sunday.*

June 2, 1984: *Saturday was the first day of the novena to prepare for Pentecost (as called for through Jelena).* Dear children, this evening I wish to say: in the days of this novena, pray for the outpouring of the Holy Spirit on all your families and your parish. Pray, and you shall not regret it. God shall give you the gifts and you shall glorify Him for it until the end of your life.

June 9, 1984: *(Eve of Pentecost)* Dear children, tomorrow night (Pentecost) pray for the Spirit of Truth! — especially you from the parish. You need the Spirit of Truth in order to be able to convey the messages the way they are, without adding to them or taking away anything, the way I gave them to you. Pray that the

Holy Spirit may inspire you with the spirit of prayer, that you pray more. I, as your Mother, say that you pray too little.

June 14, 1984: *No special message was given, nor any publicly known reason for its absence.*

June 21, 1984: Pray, pray, pray! Thank you for having responded to my call.

July 5, 1984: Dear children, today I wish to tell you: pray before your every work and end your work with prayer. If you do that, God will bless you and your work. These days you have been praying too little and working too much. Pray, therefore. In prayer you will find rest. Thank you for having responded to my call.

July 12, 1984: Dear children, these days Satan is trying to thwart all my plans. Pray that his plan may not be fulfilled. I will pray to my Son, Jesus, to give you the grace that in Satan's temptations you may experience the victory of Jesus. Thank you for having responded to my call.

July 19, 1984: Dear children, these days you have been experiencing how Satan is working. I am always watching over you. I have given myself up to you and I sympathize with you even in the smallest temptations. Thank you for having responded to my call.

July 26, 1984: Dear children, today also I would like to call you to persistent prayer and penance. Let the young people of this parish be more active in their prayers. Thank you for having responded to my call.

August 2, 1984: Dear children, today I am happy and I thank you for your prayers. Pray more these days for the conversion of sinners. Thank you for having responded to my call.

August 11, 1984: Dear children, pray, because Satan is continually trying to thwart my plans. Pray with your heart and in prayer give yourselves up to Jesus.

August 14, 1984: *(Eve of the Feast of the Assumption) Ivan received an unexpected apparition during prayer at home before going to church for the evening service. He was told to relay the following message:* I ask the people to pray with me these days. Pray all the more. Fast strictly on Wednesday and Friday; say everyday at least one rosary: the joyful, sorrowful, and glorious mysteries. *Our Lady asked the parish and the people of surrounding areas especially to accept this message with a resolute will.*

August 16, 1984: Dear children, I ask you, especially you from the parish, to live according to my messages and relate them to others, whomever you meet. Thank you for having responded to my call.

August 23, 1984: Pray, pray, pray! *This cry for perseverance in prayer was presented along with a request for the people, and especially the young to keep order in the church during the Mass.*

August 30, 1984: *Our Lady makes reference in the message to the cross on the mountain. She calls for prayers at the foot of the cross.* The cross had been in God's plan when you built it. These days especially go to the mountain and pray at the foot of the cross. I need your prayers. Thank you for having responded to my call.

September 6, 1984: Dear children, without prayer there is no peace. Therefore I say to you, dear children, pray at the foot of the cross for peace. Thank you for having responded to my call.

September 13, 1984: Dear children, I continually need your prayer. You wonder what all these prayers are for. Turn around, dear children, and you will see how much ground sin has gained in this world. Therefore, pray that Jesus may win. Thank you for having responded to my call.

September 20, 1984: Dear children, today I ask you to start fasting from your heart. There are many people who fast, but only because everyone else is fasting. It has become a custom which no one wants to stop. I ask the parish to fast out of gratitude to God for having let me remain this long in this parish. Dear children, fast and pray with your heart. Thank you for having responded to my call.

September 27, 1984: Dear children, you have helped with your prayers for my plans to be fulfilled. Pray continually that they may be fulfilled to the full. I ask the families of the parish to recite the family rosary. Thank you for having responded to my call.

October 4, 1984: Dear children, today I would like to tell you that your prayers delight me, but there are those in the parish who do not pray and my heart is sad. Pray, therefore, that I may bring all your sacrifices and prayers to the Lord. Thank you for having responded to my call.

October 8, 1984: *This message was not delivered in the church, but was received by Jakov at his house.* Dear children, let all the prayers which you say in your houses in the evening be for the conversion of sinners, because the world is in great sin. Pray the rosary every evening.

October 11, 1984: *The "testing" referred to in this message concerns a long rain in the middle of the local harvest season which caused great ruin to the crop harvest.* Dear children, thank you for offering all your pains to God, even now when He is testing you through the fruits which you are reaping. Be aware, dear children, that He loves you and, for that reason He tests you. Always present your burdens to God and do not worry. Thank you for having responded to my call.

October 18, 1984: Dear children, today I ask you to read the Bible in your houses every day and let it be in a visible place in the house so that it always encourages you to read it and pray. Thank you for having responded to my call.

October 25, 1984: Dear children, pray during this month. God gave me this month. I give it to you. Pray and ask for the graces of God. I will pray that He gives them to you. Thank you for having responded to my call.

November 1, 1984: Dear children, today I urge you to renew your prayer in your homes. Your work is finished. You must now devote yourselves to prayer.

Prayer should be at the first place in your families. Thank you for having responded to my call.

November 8, 1984: Dear children, you are not aware of the messages which God is sending to you through me. He is givng you great graces and you are not grasping them. Pray to the Holy Spirit for enlightenment — if you only knew how great are the graces God is giving you, you would pray without ceasing. Thank you for having responded to my call.

November 15, 1984: Dear children, you are a chosen people and God gave you great graces. You are not aware of every message I am giving you. Now I only wish to tell you, 'pray, pray, pray!' I do not know what else to tell you because I love you and I wish that you, in prayer, would come to know my love and the love of God. Thank you for having responded to my call.

November 22, 1984: Dear children, these days live all the messages and keep rooting them in your hearts this week. Thank you for having responded to my call.

November 29, 1984: Dear children, you do not know how to love, and you do not know how to listen with love to the words I give you. Be aware, my beloved ones, that I am your Mother and that I am coming upon earth to teach you to listen out of love and to pray out of love, and to carry your cross, but not by force. Through the cross, God is glorified in every man. Thank you for having responded to my call.

December 6, 1984: Dear children, these days I am calling you to family prayer. In God's name, many times I have given you messages, but you will not listen. This Christmas will be unforgettable for you if you will only accept the messages I am giving you. Dear children, do not allow that day of joy to be a day of greatest sorrow for me. Thank you for having responded to my call.

December 13, 1984: Dear children, you know that the day of joy is coming, but without love you cannot succeed in doing anything. Therefore, begin first by loving your own family, everyone in the parish, and then you will be able to love and accept all those who are coming here. This week must be the week in which you must learn how to love. Thank you for having responded to my call.

December 20, 1984: Dear children, today I wish you to do something concrete for Jesus. I desire that every family of the parish offer a flower for the day of joy, as a sign of their abandoment to Jesus. I desire that every member of the family has a flower near the crib (manger in the church) so that Jesus may come and see your devotion to Him. Thank you for having responded to my call.

December 27, 1984: Dear children, this Christmas Satan wanted in a special way to thwart God's plans. But you, dear children, have recognized him on the day of Christmas. God overcame him in all your hearts. Let your heart then be filled continuously with joy. Thank you for having responded to my call.

January 3, 1985: Dear children, in these days God has granted you many precious graces. Let this week be a week of thanksgiving for the graces God has granted you. Thank you for having responded to my call.

January 10, 1985: Dear children, today I want to thank you for all your sacrifices, and I especially thank those who have become dear to my heart and come here gladly. There are many parishioners who are not listening to the messages. But because of those who are in a special way close to my heart, I give messages to the parish. And I will continue giving them for I love you, and wish you to spread them by your hearts. Thank you for having responded to my call.

January 17, 1985: Dear children, in these days Satan is fighting deviously against the parish, and you, dear children, are asleep in prayer, and only some are going to Mass. Persevere in these days of temptations. Thank you for having responded to my call.

January 24, 1985: Dear children, today you have savored the sweetness of God through the renewal in your parish. Satan is working even more violently to take away the joy from each one of you. Through prayer you can totally disarm him and insure happiness. Thank you for having responded to my call.

January 31, 1985: Dear children, today I wish to tell you to open your hearts to God, like flowers in spring yearning for the sun. I am your Mother, and I always want you to be closer to the Father, and that He will always give abundant gifts to your hearts. Thank you for having responded to my call.

February 7, 1985: Dear children, Satan is manifesting himself in this parish in a particular way these days. Pray, dear children, that God's plan is carried out, and that every work of Satan is turned for the glory of God. I have remained this long to help you in your great trials. Thank you for having responded to my call.

February 14, 1985: Dear children, today is the day when I give you the message for the parish, but the whole parish is not accepting the messages and does not live them. I am sad, and I wish you, dear children, to listen to me and to live my messages. Every family must pray family prayer and read the Bible! Thank you for having responded to my call.

February 21, 1985: Dear children, from day to day I have been appealing to you for renewal and prayer in the parish, but you are not accepting it. Today I am appealing to you for the last time! This is the season of Lent, and you as a parish in Lent can be moved, for the sake of love, to my call. If you do not do that, I do not wish to give you messages that God has permitted me. Thank you for having responded to my call.

February 28, 1985: Dear children, today I call you to live the word this week: I love God! Dear children, with love you will achieve everything, and even what you think is impossible. God wants this parish to belong to Him completely, and I want that too. Thank you for having responded to my call.

March 7, 1985: Dear children, today I invite you to renew prayer in your families. Dear children, encourage the very young to pray and to go to Holy Mass. Thank you for having responded to my call.

March 14, 1985: Dear children, in your life you have all experienced light and darkness. God gives to each person knowledge of good and evil. I am calling you to the light, which you have to carry to all people who are in darkness. From day to day, people who are in darkness come to your homes. Give them, dear children, the light. Thank you for having responded to my call.

March 21, 1985: Dear children, I want to give you the message and, therefore, today, also, I call you to live and to accept my messages! Dear children, I love you, and in a special way I have chosen this parish, which is more dear to me than others where I have gladly been when the Almighty sent me. I call to you, accept me, dear children, for your well-being. Follow the messages! Thank you for having responded to my call.

March 24, 1985: *(Eve of the Annunciation)* Dear children, today I wish to call you to Confession, even if you had Confession a few days ago. I wish you to experience my feast day within yourselves. You cannot, unless you give yourselves to God completely. And so, I am calling you to reconciliation with God! Thank you for having responded to my call.

March 28, 1985: Dear children, today I want to call you — pray, pray, pray! In prayer you will come to know the greatest joy and the way out of every situation that has no way out. Thank you for moving ahead in prayer. Every individual is dear to my heart. And I thank all of you who have rekindled prayer in your families. Thank you for having responded to my call.

April 4, 1985: *(Holy Thursday)* Dear children, I thank you because you are beginning to think of the glory of God in your hearts. Today is the day when I wished to stop giving the messages because some individuals did not accept me. The parish has responded, and I wish to continue giving you the messages, like never before in history since the beginning of time. Thank you for having responded to my call.

April 5, 1985: *(Good Friday)* Dear children, you, the parishioners, have a great heavy cross, but do not be afraid to carry it. My Son is with you and He will help you. Thank you for having responded to my call.

April 11, 1985: Dear children, today I wish to say to everyone in the parish to pray in a special way for the enlightenment of the Holy Spirit. From today God wants to try the parish in a special way in order that He might strengthen it in faith. Thank you for having responded to my call.

April 18, 1985: Dear children, today I want to thank you for every opening of your hearts. Joy overwhelms me for every heart that opens to God, especially in the parish. Rejoice with me! Pray all the prayers for the opening of sinful hearts. I want this. God wants this through me. Thank you for having responded to my call.

April 25, 1985: Dear children, today I want to tell you to begin to work in your hearts as you work in the fields. Work and change your hearts so that the Spirit of God moves in your heart. Thank you for having responded to my call.

May 2, 1985: Dear children, today I invite you to prayer of the heart, and not only habit. Some are coming but do not move in prayer. Therefore, I beg you as a Mother, pray that prayer prevails in your heart in every moment. Thank you for having responded to my call.

May 9, 1985: Dear children, you do not know how many graces God is giving you. These days when the Holy Spirit is working in a special way, you do not want to advance; your hearts are turned towards earthly things, and you are occupied by them. Turn your hearts to prayer and ask that the Holy Spirit be poured upon you. Thank you for having responded to my call.

May 16, 1985: Dear children, I am calling you to more attentive prayer, and more participation in the Mass. I wish you to experience God within yourself during Mass. I wish to say to the youth, especially, be open to the Holy Spirit, because God wants to draw you to Himself these days when Satan is active. Thank you for having responded to my call.

May 23, 1985: Dear children, open your hearts to the Holy Spirit in a special way these days. The Holy Spirit is working in a special way through you. Open your hearts and give your lives to Jesus, so that He may work through your hearts and strengthen you. Thank you for having responded to my call.

May 30, 1985: I am calling you again to prayer of the heart. Let prayer, dear children, be your every day food. In a special way now when work in the fields is exhausting you, you cannot pray with your heart. Pray, and then you will overcome every tiredness. Prayer will be your happiness and rest. Thank you for having responded to my call.

June 6, 1985: Dear children, in these days many people of all nationalities will come to the parish. And now I am telling you to love. Love, first of all, members of your own family, and then you might be able to accept in love all those who are coming. Thank you for having responded to my call.

June 13, 1985: Dear children, until the anniversary day (June 25) I am calling you, you in the parish, to pray more, and let your prayer be a sign of your surrender to God. Dear children, I know about your tiredness. But you don't know how to surrender yourselves to me. These days, surrender yourselves to me completely. Thank your for having responded to my call.

June 20, 1985: Dear children, I wish on this feast day for you to open you hearts to the Lord of all hearts. Give me all you feelings and all your problems. I wish to console you in all your temptations. I wish to fill you with the peace, joy and love of God. Thank you for having responded to my call.

June 25, 1985: Dear children, I ask you to ask everyone to pray the rosary. With the rosary you will overcome all the troubles which Satan is trying to inflict on the Catholic Church. *Our Lady gave this message to Mirjana when she asked: "Madonna, what do you wish to say to priests?"*: "Let all priests pray the rosary. Give time to the rosary." Thank you for having responded to my call.

June 27, 1985: Dear children, today I give you the message through which I am calling you to humility. These days you have felt great joy because of all the people who are coming, and you have spoken about your experiences with love. Now I call you to continue in humility and with an open heart to speak to all those who are coming. Thank you for having responded to my call.

July 4, 1985: Dear children, thank you for every sacrifice you have offered. Now I urge you to offer every sacrifice with love. I desire that you who are helpless begin with trust. The Lord will give to you always if you trust. Thank you for having responded to my call.

July 11, 1985: Dear children, I love this parish and I protect it with my mantle from every work of Satan. Pray that Satan flees from this parish and from every individual that comes to the parish. In this way you will be able to hear every call and answer it with your life. Thank you for having responded to my call.

July 18, 1985: Dear children, today I beg you to put more blessed objects in your homes, and carry blessed objects. Let everything be blessed so that Satan will tempt you less because you are armed against him. Thank you for having responded to my call.

July 25, 1985: Dear children, I want to shepherd you, but you do not want to obey my messages. Today I call you to obey my messages. Then you will be able to live everything that God tells me to tell you. Open yourselves to God, and God will work through you and give you everything you need. Thank you for having responded to my call.

August 1, 1985: Dear children, I wish to tell you that I have chosen this parish. I protect it, holding it in my hands like a fragile little flower that struggles for life. I beg you to give yourselves to me so that I can offer you clean and without sin as a gift to God. Satan has taken one part of the plan, and he wants to have it all. Pray that he does not succeed, because I desire to have you for myself to offer you to God. Thank you for having responded to my call.

August 8, 1985: Dear children, today I call you to pray against Satan in a special way. Satan wants to work more now that you know he is active. Dear children, put on your armor against Satan; with rosaries in your hands you will conquer. Thank you for having responded to my call.

August 15, 1985: *(Feast of the Assumption)* Dear children, today I bless you, and I want to tell you that I love you. I appeal to you in this moment to live my messages. Today I bless you with a solemn blessing that the Almighty grants me to give. Thank you for having responded to my call.

August 22, 1985: Dear children, today I wish to tell you that God wants to send you tests which you can overcome with prayer. God is testing you through your everyday work. Now pray that you may overcome every temptation peacefully. Come through every test from God more open to Him, and come to Him with love. Thank you for having responded to my call.

August 29, 1985: Dear children, I call you to prayer especially now when Satan wants to make use of the grapes of your vineyards. Pray that he does not succeed. Thank you for having responded to my call.

September 5, 1985: Dear children, today I thank you for all your prayers. Keep on praying so that Satan will stay far away from this place. Dear children, the plan of Satan has failed. Pray that everything God plans for this village becomes reality. In a special way I want to thank the young people for all the sacrifices they have offered. Thank you for having responded to my call.

September 12, 1985: Dear children, I want to ask you in these days to put the cross in the center. Pray in a special way before the cross; many graces come from the cross. Make a special consecration to the holy cross in your homes. Promise that you will not offend Jesus nor offend against the cross, and that you will not blaspheme. Thank you for having responded to my call.

September 19, 1985: Dear children, today I ask you to live in humility all the messages I give you. Dear children, do not become proud living the messages, saying in your hearts, "I live the messages!" If you bear the messages in your heart and if you live them, then everyone will feel it and there will be no need for words; words are used only by those who do not listen. It is not necessary for you to speak with words. For you, dear children, it is necessary only to live the message and to witness with your lives. Thank you for having responded to my call.

September 26, 1985: Dear children, I thank you for all your prayers. Thank you for all the sacrifices. I wish to tell you, dear children, to renew living the messages that I have given you. In particular, live the messages regarding fasting, because your fasting gives me joy. And so you will attain the fulfillment of all the plans that God has for you here in Medjugorje. Thank you for having responded to my call.

October 3, 1985: Dear children, I ask you to give thanks to God for all the graces that He gives you. Give thanks to God for all the fruits of His grace, and praise Him. Dear children, learn how to give thanks for little things, and then you will be able to give thanks for great things. Thank you for having responded to my call.

October 10, 1985: Dear children, again today I want to call you to live the messages in the parish. Especially, I want to call the young people of the parish, because this parish is beloved to me. Dear children, if you are living the messages, you live the seed of holiness. As a Mother, I want to call all of you to holiness so that you can give it to others, because you are like mirrors to other people. Thank you for having responded to my call.

October 17, 1985: Dear children, everything has its time. Today I invite you to begin working on your hearts. All the work in the field is finished. You found the time to clean out the most abandoned places, but you have neglected your hearts. Work hard and clean up every part of your heart with love. Thank you for having responded to my call.

October 24, 1985: Dear children, I want to dress you from day to day in holiness, goodness, obedience, and the love of God, so that from day to day you can be more beautiful and better prepared for your Lord. Dear children, listen to my messages and live them. I desire to lead you! Thank you for having responded to my call.

October 31, 1985: Dear children, today I wish to call you to work in the Church. I do love you equally. I want you to work as much as you can in the Church. I know, dear children, that you can work, but you do not want to work because you feel that you are unworthy of the duties. You have to be courageous. With the little flower you enrich the Church and Jesus so that we can all be happy. Thank you for having responded to my call.

November 7, 1985: Dear children, I am calling you to love your neighbors, to love those people from whom the evil is coming to you, and so in the power of love you will be able to judge the intentions of the heart. Pray and love, dear children; in the power of love you can do even those things that seem impossible to you. Thank you for having responded to my call.

November 14, 1985: Dear children, I, your Mother, love you, and I wish to urge you to prayer. I am, dear children, tireless, and I call you even when you are far away from my heart. I feel pain for everyone who has gone astray. But I am a mother and I forgive easily, and I rejoice for every child who comes back to me. Thank you for having responded to my call.

November 21, 1985: Dear children, I wish to tell you that this time is special for you who are from the parish. In the summer you say that you have a lot of work to do. Now there is no work in the fields: work on yourselves personally. Come to the Mass because this time has been given to you. Dear children, there are many of those who come regularly in spite of bad weather because they love me and they wish to show their love in a special way. I ask you to show me your love by coming to the Mass, and the Lord will reward you abundantly. Thank you for having responded to my call.

November 28, 1985: Dear children, I want to give thanks to all for all they have done for me, especially the young ones. I beg you, dear children, to come to prayer consciously, and in prayer you will know the majesty of God. Thank you for having responded to my call.

December 5, 1985: Dear children, I call you to prepare yourselves for Christmas by penance, prayer and works of charity. Don't look at the material, because then you will not be able to experience Christmas. Thank you for having responded to my call.

December 12, 1985: Dear children, for Christmas I invite you to give glory to Jesus together with me. I will give Him to you in a special way on that day, I invite you is on that day to give glory and praise with me to Jesus at His birth. Dear children, pray more on that day and think more about Jesus. Thank you for having responded to my call.

December 19, 1985: Dear children, I want to invite you to love your neighbor. If you love your neighbor you will experience Jesus' love more, especially on Christmas day. God will give you a great gift if you abandon yourselves to Him. I want to give to mothers, in particular on Christmas day, my maternal blessing, and I will bless the others with His blessings. Thank you for having responded to my call.

December 26, 1985: Dear children, I want to thank all of you who have listened to my messages and who have lived on Christmas Day what I have told you. I want to guide you. Put aside your sins. From now on go forward in love. Abandon your heart to me. Thank you for having responded to my call! *On Christmas day, Our Lady was reported to have appeared with the Baby Jesus.*

January 2, 1986: Dear children, I invite you to decide completely for God. I beg you, dear children, to surrender yourselves completely and you will be able to live everything I say to you. Thank you for having responded to my call.

January 9, 1986: Dear children, I invite you to prayer so that with your prayers you will help Jesus to realize all the plans that are here. By offerings and sacrifices to Jesus, everything will be fulfilled that is planned. Satan can not do anything. Thank you for having responded to my call.

January 16, 1986: Dear children, I invite you to pray. I need your prayers so much in order that God may be glorified through all of you. Dear children, I beg you to listen and live your Mother's call, because I am calling you by reason of my love for you so that I can help you. Thank you for having responded to my call.

January 23, 1986: Dear children, again I invite you to prayer of the heart. If you pray from your heart, dear children, the ice cold hearts of your brothers will be melted and every barrier will disappear. Conversion will be easily achieved by those who want it. You must intercede for this gift for your neighbors. Thank you for having responded to my call.

January 30, 1986: Dear children, today I invite all of you to pray in order that God's plans with you and all that God wills through you may be realized. Help others to be converted, especially those who are coming to Medjugorje. Dear children, do not allow Satan to reign in your hearts. Do not be an image of Satan, but my image. I am calling you to pray so that may be witnesses of my presence. God cannot fulfill His will without you. God gave everyone free will and it is up to you to be disposed. Thank you for having responded to my call.

February 6, 1986: Dear children, this parish is elected by me and is special. It is different from others, and I am giving great graces to all who are praying from their hearts. Dear children, I am giving you my messages, first of all, for the parish, and then for all others. The messages are first of all for you, and then for others who will accept them. You will be responsible to me and to my Son, Jesus. Thank you for having responded to my call.

February 13, 1986: Dear children, this Lent is a special incentive for you to change. Start from this moment. Turn off the television and renounce other things which are useless. Dear children, I am calling you individually to convert. This time is for you. Thank you for having responded to my call.

February 20, 1986: Dear children, the second message for Lenten days is that you renew your prayer before the cross. Dear children, I am giving you special graces and Jesus is giving you special gifts from the cross. Accept them and live them. Reflect on Jesus' Passion and unite yourselves to Jesus in life. Thank you for having responded to my call.

February 27, 1986: Dear children, be humble, live in humility. Thank you for having responded to my call.

March 6, 1986: Dear children, today I am calling you to open yourselves more to God so that He can work through you. For as much as you open yourselves, you will receive the fruits from it. I wish to call you again to prayer. Thank you for having responded to my call.

March 13, 1986: Dear children, today I am calling you to live this Lent with your little sacrifices. Thank you for every sacrifice you have brought to me. Dear children, live in such a way continuously and with love. Help me to bring offerings of your sacrifices to God for which He will reward you. Thank you for having responded to my call.

March 20, 1986: Dear children, today I am calling you to an active approach to prayer. You wish to live everything I am telling you, but you do not have results from your efforts because you do not pray. Dear children, I beg you to open yourselves and begin to pray. Prayer will be joy. If you begin, it will not be boring, because you will pray out of pure joy. Thank you for having responded to my call.

March 27, 1986: *(Holy Thursday)* Dear children, I wish to thank you for your sacrifices and I invite you to the greatest sacrifice, the sacrifice of love. Without love you are not able to accept me or my Son. Without love you cannot witness your experience to others. That is why I invite you, dear children, to begin to live the love in your hearts. Thank you for having responded to my call.

April 3, 1986: Dear children, I wish to call you to live the Holy Mass. There are many of you who have experienced the beauty of the Mass, but there are also some who come unwillingly. I have chosen you, dear children, and Jesus is giving you His graces in the Holy Mass. Therefore, live consciously the Holy Mass. Let every coming to Holy Mass be joyful. Come with love and accept the Holy Mass. Thank you for having responded to my call.

April 10, 1986: Dear children, I wish to call you to grow in love. A flower cannot grow without water. Neither can you grow without God's blessings. You should pray for blessings from day to day so that you can grow up normally and carry out your activities with God. Thank you for having responded to my call.

April 17, 1986: Dear children, now you are preoccupied about material things, and in the material you lose everything that God wants to give you. I am inviting you, dear children, to pray for the gifts of the Holy Spirit that you need now in order that you may witness my presence here and in everything I am giving you. Dear children, abandon yourselves to me so that I can lead you totally. Do not be so preoccupied about the material things of this world. Thank you for having responded to my call.

April 24, 1986: Dear children, today I am calling you to prayer. You are forgetting that everyone is important, especially the elderly in the family. Incite them to pray. Let all the youth be an example by their lives and testify for Jesus. Dear children, I beg you to start transforming yourselves through prayer, and then you will know what you have to do. Thank you for having responded to my call.

May 1, 1986: Dear children, I ask you to begin to change your life in your families. Let your family be a harmonious flower which I wish to give to Jesus. Dear children, every family should be active in prayer. It is my wish that the fruits of prayer will be seen one day in the family. Only in that way will I give you as petals to Jesus in fulfillment of God's plan. Thank you for having responded to my call.

May 8, 1986: *(Ascension Thursday)* Dear children, you are responsible for the messages. The source of grace is here, but you, dear children, are the vehicles transmitting the gifts. Therefore, dear children, I am calling you to work responsibly. Everyone will be responsible according to his own measure. Dear children, I am calling you to give the gifts to others with love and not to keep it for yourselves. Thank you for having responded to my call.

May 15, 1986: Dear children, today I am calling you to give me your heart so I can change it to be like mine. You are asking yourselves, dear children, why you cannot respond to what I am seeking from you. You cannot because you have not given me your heart so I can change it. You are seeking, but not acting. I call you to do everything I tell you; in that way I will be with you. Thank you for having responded to my call.

May 22, 1986: Dear children, today I will give you my love. You don't know, dear children, how great my love is, and you don't know how to accept it. In many ways I wish to express it but you, dear children, do not recognize it. You don't comprehend my words by your heart, and so you are not able to comprehend my love. Dear children, accept me in your life, and so you will be able to accept all I am saying to you and I am calling you for. Thank you for having responded to my call.

May 29, 1986: Dear children, today I am calling you to a life of love towards God and your neighbor. Without love, dear children, you cannot do anything. Therefore, dear children, I am calling you to live in mutual love. Only in that way can you love me and accept everyone around you coming to your parish. Everyone will feel my love through you. Therefore, today I beg you to start loving with a burning love. Thank you for having responded to my call.

June 5, 1986: Dear children, today I am calling you to decide if you wish to live the messages I am giving you. I wish you to be active in living and transmitting the messages. Especially, dear children, I desire you to be the reflection of Jesus who enlightens an unfaithful world which is walking in darkness. I wish that all of you may be a light to all and witness to the light. Dear children, you are not called to the darkness; you are called to the light and to live the light in your life. Thank you for having responded to my call.

June 12, 1986: Dear children, today I am begging you to pray the rosary with lively faith. Only this way can I help you. Pray. I cannot help you because you don't want to be moved. Dear children, I am calling you to pray the rosary. The rosary should be your commitment, prayed by you with joy and so you will understand why I am visiting you for such a long time. I want to teach you to pray. Thank you for having responded to my call.

June 19, 1986: Dear children, in these days the Lord has allowed me to intercede for more graces for you. Therefore, dear children, I want to urge you once again to prayer. Pray constantly, and in this way I will give you the joy which the Lord gives me. With these graces, dear children, I want your sufferings to be for you a joy. I am your Mother, and I want to help you. Thank you for having responded to my call.

June 24-25, 1986: *(The Anniversary) On the anniversary Our Lady said that she was giving special blessings to all who had come and to all who were associated with Medjugorje.*

On the evening of the 24th Our Lady appeared on the mountaintop to Marija and Ivan, where a group of people had gathered. Marija said she recommended everyone to the Madonna. The Virgin blessed everyone and said: Continue to pray here. Pray the rosary again. *She (Our Lady) said that this Tabor is for everyone and that we should bring this Tabor experience to all our homes. With this Tabor we must bring peace and reconciliation. Marija said that Our Lady appeared with five angels and that she was very happy.*

June 26, 1986: Dear children, God allowed me to bring about this oasis of peace. I want to invite you to guard it and let the oasis remain pure always. There are those who are destroying peace and prayer by their carelessness. I am calling you to witness and, by your life, preserve the peace. Thank you for having responded to my call.

July 3, 1986: Dear children, today I am calling you to prayer. Without prayer you cannot feel me, nor God, nor the graces I am giving you. Therefore, I call you always to begin and end each day with prayer. Dear children, I wish to lead you evermore in prayer, but you cannot grow because you don't want it. I invite you to let prayer have the first place. Thank you for having responded to my call.

July 10, 1986: Dear children, today I invite you to holiness. You cannot live without holiness. Consequently, overcome all sin with love. Overcome every difficulty you meet with love. Dear children, I beg you to live love within yourselves. Thank you for having responded to my call.

July 17, 1986: Dear children, today I invite you to meditate on why I am with you for such a long time. I am the mediator between you and God. For that reason,

I would like to invite you to live always, out of love, what God is expecting from you. Dear children, live all the messages that I give you in complete humilit. Thank you for having responded to my call.

July 24, 1986: Dear children, I am happy about all of you who are on the way of holiness, and I am begging you to help all those with your witness who don't know how to live in the way of holiness. For that reason, dear children, your families should be the place where holiness is born. Help everybody to live in a sanctified way, especially your own family. Thank you for having responded to my call.

July 31, 1986: Dear children, hatred creates division and does not see anybody or anything. I invite you always to carry unity and peace. Especially, dear children, act with love in the place where you live. Let love always be your only tool. With love turn everything to good that the devil wants to destroy and take to himself. Only this way will you be completely mine and I will be able to help you. Thank you for having responded to my call.

August 7, 1986: Dear children, you know I promised you an oasis of peace here, but you are not aware that around every oasis is a desert where Satan is lurking. He wants to tempt each one of you. Dear children, only by prayer are you able to overcome every influence of Satan in your place. I am with you, but I can't take away your free will. Thank you for having responded to my call.

August 14, 1986: Dear children, I am inviting you so that your prayer may be a joyful encounter with the Lord. I cannot guide you unless you yourself experience joy in prayer. I want to guide you in prayer more and more, from day to day, but I do not want to force you. Thank you for having responded to my call.

August 21, 1986: Dear children, I am grateful for the love you are showing me. Dear children, you know that I am loving you without limit, and that I am praying daily to the Lord so that He may help you understand the love I am showing you. Therefore, dear children, pray and pray and pray!

August 28, 1986: Dear children, I call you to be a picture to everyone and everything especially in prayer and witnessing. Dear children, I cannot help the world without you. I want you to cooperate with me in everything, even in the smallest things, by your prayer from your heart and by surrendering to me completely. Dear children, help me. In that way I will be able to teach you and to lead you on this road which I began with you. Thank you for having responded to my call.

September 4, 1986: Dear children, today again I am calling you to prayer and fasting. You know, dear children, with your help I can do everything and force Satan not to seduce people to evil and to remove him from this place. Satan, dear children, watches for every individual. He wants particularly to bring confusion to every one of you. Dear children, I ask that your every day becomes prayer and complete surrender to God. Thank you for having responded to my call.

September 11, 1986: Dear children, for these days when you celebrate the cross with joy, I wish your cross to be joyful. Dear children, pray that you can accept sickness and suffering with love like Jesus. Only that way can I give you the graces of healing with the joy that Jesus allows. Thank you for having responded to my call.

September 18, 1986: Dear children, today again I am grateful for everything you have done for me in these days. I am thanking you in the name of Jesus especially for the sacrifices you offered in the last week. Dear children, you are forgetting that I want sacrifices from you to help you and to banish Satan. Therefore, I am calling you again to offer sacrifices with special reverence towards God. Thank you for having responded to my call.

September 25, 1986: Dear children, through your own peace, I am calling you to help others to see and to start searching for peace. Dear children, you are at peace and, therefore, you cannot comprehend the absence of peace. Again I am calling you so that through prayer and your life you will help destroy everything evil in people and uncover the deception which Satan is using. Pray for truth to prevail in every heart. Thank you for having responded to my call.

October 2, 1986: Dear children, today again I invite you to prayer. You, dear children, do not realize the preciousness of prayer. Now is the time of prayer. Now, nothing else is important. Now, nobody is important except God. Dear children, dedicate yourselves to prayer with special love. Only in that way can God give you graces. Thank you for having responded to my call.

October 9, 1986: Dear children, you know that I wish to guide you on the way of holiness, but I do not want to force you. I do not want you to be holy by force. I wish everyone of you to help yourselves and me by your little sacrifices so that I can guide you to be more holy day by day. Therefore, dear children, I do not want to force you to live the messages; but rather this long time I am with you shows that I love you immeasurably and that I wish every single one of you to be holy. Thank you for having responded to my call.

October 16, 1986: Dear children, today, also I want to show you how much I love you. I am sorry that I am not able to help each and every one of you to fathom my love. Therefore, dear children, I am calling you to prayer and complete surrender to God, because Satan wants to conquer you in everyday affairs. He wants to take the first place in your life. Pray, dear children, without ceasing. Thank you for having responded to my call.

October 23, 1986: Dear children, today I invite you to pray. I give you a special invitation, dear children, to pray for peace. Without your prayers, my dear children, I cannot help you to understand what my Lord has given me to give to you. Therefore, dear children, pray that peace would be given to you by God. Thank you for having responded to my call.

October 30, 1986: Dear children, today, also, I want to call you to take seriously and live the messages which I am giving you. Dear children, because of you I have remained this long to help you to put into practice all the messages which I am giving you. Therefore, dear children, out of love for me live all the messages which I am giving you. Thank you for having responded to my call.

November 6, 1986: Today, I would like to invite you to pray day by day for the souls in purgatory. Every soul needs prayer and grace to reach God and His love. With this, you too, dear children, will find new intercessors who will help you in life to know that all the things of this earth are not important to you. The only one you have to turn to is in Heaven. For this reason, dear children, pray without interruption so that you might help yourselves and those whom prayer gives you. Thank you for having responded to my call.

November 13, 1986: Dear children, today, also, I call you to pray with your whole heart and to change your life day by day. Especially, I am calling you, dear children, by your prayers and sacrifices. Begin to live in holiness, because I want every one of you who has been here at this spring of graces to come to Heaven with a special gift for me, this gift of holiness. Therefore, dear children, pray daily and change your life in order that you may be holy. I will always be close to you. Thank you for having responded to my call.

November 20, 1986: Dear children, today, also I am calling you to live and to pay attention with a special love to all the messages I am giving you. God does not want you lukewarm and indecisive, but totally committed to Him. You know that I love you and that I am burning out of love for you. Therefore, dear children, commit yourselves to love so that you will comprehend and burn with God's love from day to day. Decide for love, dear children, so that love may prevail in all of you — not human love, but God's love. Thank you for having responded to my call.

November 27, 1986: Dear children, today, also, I invite you to dedicate your life to me with love, in order that I can guide you with love. I love you, dear children, with a special love, and I want to bring you to Heaven to God. I want you to comprehend that this life is very short in comparison with that in Heaven. Therefore, dear children, today decide anew for God. Only in that way can I show how much you are beloved to me and how much I want all of you to be saved and to be with me in Heaven. Thank you for having responded to my call.

December 4, 1986: Dear children, today, also, I invite you to prepare your hearts for these days when the Lord is about to purify you in a special way from all the sins of your past life. You, dear children, cannot do it by yourselves, and for that reason I am here to help you. Pray, dear children. Only in that way will you be able to recognize all the evil that dwells in you, and abandon it to the Lord so that He may purify your hearts completely. So, dear children, pray without ceasing and prepare your hearts in penance and fasting. Thank you for having responded to my call.

December 11, 1986: Dear children, I invite you especially to pray during this season so that you may experience the joy of meeting the new-born Jesus. Dear children, I desire that you experience these days just as I experience them with joy. I wish to guide you and show you the joy which I want to bring to all of you. Therefore, dear children, pray and surrender yourselves completely to me. Thank you for having responded to my call.

December 18, 1986: Dear children, once again today I want to invite you to pray. When you pray, dear children, you become like flowers which, after the snow, show forth their beauty, and whose colors become indescribable. And so you, dear children, after prayer before God, display everything that is beautiful so that you may become beloved by Him. Therefore, dear children, pray and open your inner self to the Lord so that He may make of you a harmonious and beautiful flower for Heaven. Thank you for having responded to my call.

December 25, 1986: Dear children, today, also, I am grateful to my Lord for all He is giving me, especially for this gift of being with you again today.

Dear children, these are the days in which the Father is giving special graces to all who open their hearts. I am blessing you. My desire, dear children, is that you may recognize God's graces and place everything at His disposal so that He may be glorified by you. My heart follows all your steps attentively. Thank you for having responded to my call.

January 1, 1987: Dear children, today I want to call you to live the messages I am giving you in the New Year. Dear children, you know that for your sake I have remained so long so as to teach you how to walk on the road of holiness. Therefore, dear children, pray without ceasing and live the messages I am giving you, for I do it with great love towards God and you. Thank you for having responded to my call.

January 8, 1987: Dear children, I want to thank you for every response to my messages. Especially, dear children, thank you for all the sufferings and prayers you have offered to me. Dear children, I want to give you messages no longer every Thursday, but on the 25th of each month. The time has come when what my Lord wanted has been fulfilled. From now on I will give you fewer messages, but I will be with you. Therefore, dear children, I beg you to listen to my messages and to live them so that I can guide you. Thank you for having responded to my call.

Monthly Messages

January 25, 1987: Dear children, today I want to call you to begin to live the new life from today onwards. Dear children, I want you to comprehend that God has chosen each one of you, in order to use you for the great plan of salvation of mankind. You cannot comprehend how great your role is in God's plan. Therefore, dear children, pray, so that through prayer you may comprehend God's plan through you. I am with you so that you realize it completely. Thank you for having responded to my call.

February 25, 1987: Dear children, today I would like to envelop you with my mantle and lead you toward the road to resurrection. Dear children, I beg you to give our Lord your past and all the evil that has accumulated in your hearts. I want all of you to be happy, and with sin no one can be happy. That is why, dear children, you must pray, and in your prayers you will realize the path to holiness. Happiness will be in your heart and you will be the witness to that which I and My Son want for all of you. I bless you, dear children. Thank you for having responded to my call.

March 25, 1987: Dear children, today I want to thank you for your presence in this place where I give special graces. I call upon each one of you to start living the life which God wants from you, and to start doing good deeds of love and generosity. I do not want you, dear children, to live the message while committing the sins which I do not like. Therefore, dear children, I want each of you live the new life without destroying everything God creates in you and gives you. I give you my special blessings and remain with you on your way to conversion. Thank you for having responded to my call.

April 25, 1987: Dear children, today also I am inviting you to prayer. In all, dear children, God is granting special graces in prayer. Therefore, dear children, seek and pray in order that you may be able to understand all that I am giving you in this place. I am calling you, dear children, to pray with your heart. You know, dear children, that without prayer you cannot comprehend all that God is planning through each one of you — and so, pray. I desire that through every one of you God's plan may be fulfilled, that all God has given you in your hearts may increase. Therefore, pray that God's blessing may protect every one of you from all the evil that is threatening you. I am begging you, dear children. Thank you for having responded to my call.

May 25, 1987: Dear children, I invite everyone of you to start living in God's love. Dear children, you are ready to commit sin and to put yourselves in the hand of Satan without reflecting. I invite every one of you to decide consciously for God and against Satan. I am your Mother and want to lead you all towards perfect holiness. I want every one of you to be happy here on earth, and I want every one of you to be with me in Heaven. This is, dear children, the reason for my coming here and my desire for you. Thank you for having responded to my call.

June 25, 1987: Dear children, today I thank you and I want to invite you all to God's peace. I want each of you to experience in your heart the peace that God gives. Today I want to bless all of you. I am blessing you with God's blessing. I beg you, dear children, to follow and to live my way. I love you, dear children, and therefore, I am calling you again and I am thanking you for all that you are doing for my intentions. I beg you to help me to present you to God, to save you and lead you on the way of salvation. Thank you for having responded to my call.

July 25, 1987: Dear children, I beseech you to take up the way of holiness, beginning today. I love you and, therefore, I want you to be holy. I do not want Satan to block you on that way. Dear children, pray and accept all that God is offering you on a way which is bitter. But at the same time, God will reveal every sweetness to whomever begins to go on that way, and he or she will gladly answer every call from God. Do not attribute importance to petty things. Long for Heaven. Thank you for having responded to my call.

August 25, 1987: Dear children, today also I am inviting you all so that each one of you decides to live my messages. God has permitted me, also, in this year which the Church has dedicated to me, to be able to speak to you and to be able to spur you on to holiness. Dear children, seek from God the graces which He is giving you through me. I am ready to intercede with God for all that you seek so your holiness may be complete. Therefore, dear children, do not forget to seek, because God has permitted me to obtain graces for you. Thank you for having responded to my call.

September 25, 1987: Dear children, today also I want to invite all to prayer. Let prayer be life for you. Dear children, dedicate your time only to Jesus and He will give you everything that you are seeking. He will reveal Himself to you completely. Dear children, Satan is strong and is waiting to test each one of you. That way he will not be able to injure you or block you on the way to holiness. Dear children, through prayer grow all the more toward God from day to day. Thank you for having responded to my call.

October 25, 1987: My dear children, today I wish to invite all of you to decide for Paradise. The way is difficult for those who have not decided for God. Dear children, decide and believe that God is offering Himself to you in His fullness. You are invited and you need to answer the call of the Father, who is calling you through me. Pray, because in prayer each one of you will be able to achieve complete love. I am blessing you, and I desire to help you so that each one of you might be under my motherly mantle. Thank you for having responded to my call.

November 25, 1987: Dear children, today also I invite each one of you to decide to surrender again everything completely to me. Only that way will I be able to present each one of you to God. Dear children, you know that I love you immeasurably and that I desire each one of you for myself, but God has given to all a freedom which I lovingly respect and to which I humbly submit. I desire, dear children, that you help so that everything God has planned in this parish shall be realized. If you do not pray, you will not be able to recognize my love and the plans which God has for this parish and for each individual. Pray that Satan does not entice you with his pride and deceptive strength. I am with you and I want you to believe me that I love you. Thank you for having responded to my call.

December 25, 1987: Dear children, rejoice with me! My heart is rejoicing because of Jesus and I want to give Him to you. Dear children, I want each one of you to open your heart to Jesus and I will give Him to you with love. Dear children, I want Him to change you, to teach you and to protect you. Today I am praying in a special way for each one of you and I am presenting you to God so He will manifest Himself in you. I am calling you to sincere prayer with the heart so that every prayer of yours may be an encounter with God. In your work and in your everyday life, do put God in the first place. I invite you today with great seriousness to obey me and to do as I am inviting you. Thank you for having responded to my call.

January 25, 1988: Dear children, today again I am calling you to complete conversion, which is difficult for those who have not chosen God. I am inviting you, dear children, to convert fully to God. God can give you everything that you seek from Him. But you seek God only when sicknesses, problems and difficulties come to you and you think that God is far from you and is not listening and does not hear your prayers. No, dear children, that is not the truth. When you are far from God, you cannot receive graces because you do not seek them with a firm faith. Day by day, I am praying for you and I want to draw you ever more near to God, but I cannot if you don't want it. Therefore, dear children put your life in God's hands. I bless you all. Thank you for having responded to my call.

February 25, 1988: Dear children, today again I am calling you to prayer and to complete surrender to God. You know that I love you and I am coming here out of love so I could show you the path to peace and salvation for your souls. I want you to obey me and not permit Satan to seduce you. Dear children, Satan is very strong and, therefore, I ask you to dedicate your prayers to me so that those who are under his influence can be saved. Give witness by your life. Sacrifice your lives for the salvation of the world. I am with you and I am grateful to you, but in heaven you shall receive the Father's reward which He has promised to you. Therefore, little children, do not be afraid. If you pray, Satan cannot injure you even a little bit because you are God's children and He is watching over you. Pray and let the rosary always be in your hands as a sign to Satan that you belong to me. Thank you for having responded to my call.

March 25, 1988: Dear children, today also I am inviting you to a complete surrender to God. Dear children, you are not conscious of how God loves you with such a great love because He permits me to be with you so I can instruct you and help you to find the way of peace. This way, however, you cannot discover if you do not pray. Therefore, dear children, forsake everything and consecrate your time to God and then God will bestow gifts upon you and bless you. Little children, don't forget that your life is fleeting like a spring flower which today is wondrously beautiful but tomorrow has vanished. Therefore, pray in such a way that your prayer, your surrender to God, may become like a road sign. That way, your witness will not only have value for yourselves but for all eternity. Thank you for having responded to my call.

April 25, 1988: Dear children, God wants to make you holy. Therefore, through me He is inviting you to complete surrender. Let Holy Mass be your life. Understand that the church is God's palace, the place in which I gather you and want to show you the way to God. Come and pray. Neither look at others nor slander them, but rather, let your life be a testimony on the way of holiness. Churches deserve respect and are set apart as holy because God, who became man, dwells in them day and night. Therefore, little children, believe and pray that the Father increase your faith, and then ask for whatever you need. I am with you and I am rejoicing because of your conversion and I am protecting you with my motherly mantle. Thank you for having responded to my call.

May 25, 1988: Dear children, I am inviting you to a complete surrender to God. Pray, little children, that Satan may not carry you about like branches in the wind. Be strong in God. I desire that through you the whole world may get to know the God of joy. By your life bear witness for God's joy. Do not be anxious nor worried. God himself will help you and show you the way. I desire that you love all men with my love. Only in that way can love reign over the world. Little children, you are mine. I love you and want you to surrender to me so that I can lead you to God. Never cease praying so that Satan cannot take advantage of you. Pray for the knowledge that you are mine. I bless you with blessings of joy. Thank you for having responded to my call.

June 25, 1988: Dear children, I am calling you to that love which is loyal and pleasing to God. Little children, love bears everything bitter and difficult for the sake of Jesus who is Love. Therefore, dear children, pray that God comes to your aid, not however according to your desires, but according to His love. Surrender yourselves to God so that He may heal you, console you and forgive everything inside you which is a hindrance on the way of love. In this way God can mold your life, and you will grow in love. Dear children, glorify God with a canticle of love so that God's love may be able to grow in you day by day to its fullness. Thank you for having responded to my call.

July 25, 1988: Dear children, today I am calling you to a complete surrender to God. Everything you do and everything you possess give over to God so that He can take control in your life as the King of all that you possess. That way, through me, God can lead you into the depths of the spiritual life. Little children, do not be afraid, because I am with you even if you think there is no way out and that Satan is in control. I am bringing peace to you. I am your mother, the Queen of Peace. I am blessing you with the blessing of joy so that for you God may be everything in your life. Thank you for having responded to my call.

August 25, 1988: Dear children, today I invite you all to rejoice in the life which God gives you. Little children, rejoice in God, the Creator, because He has created you so wonderfully. Pray that your life be joyful thanksgiving which flows out of your heart like a river of joy. Little children, give thanks unceasingly for all that you possess, for each little gift which God has given you, so that a joyful blessing always comes down from God upon your life. Thank you for having responded to my call.

September 25, 1988: Dear children, today I am inviting all of you, without exception, to the way of holiness in your life. God gave you the grace, the gift of holiness. Pray that you may, more and more, comprehend it, and in that way, you will be able, by your life, to bear witness for God. Dear children, I am blessing you and I intercede to God for you so that your way and your witness may be a complete one and a joy for God. Thank you for having responded to my call.

October 25, 1988: Dear children, my invitation that you live the messages which I am giving you is a daily one, especially, little children, because I want to draw you closer to the Heart of Jesus. Therefore, little children, I am inviting you today to the prayer of consecration to Jesus, my dear Son, so that each of your hearts may be His. And then I am inviting you to consecration to my Immaculate Heart. I want you to consecrate yourselves as persons, as families and as parishes so that all belongs to God through my hands. Therefore, dear little children, pray that you comprehend the greatness of this message which I am giving you. I do not want anything for myself, rather all for the salvation of your souls. Satan is strong and therefore, you, little children, by constant prayer, press tightly against my motherly heart. Thank you for having responded to my call.

November 25, 1988: Dear children, I am inviting you to prayer so that in prayer you may have an encounter with God. God is offering and giving Himself to you but He seeks from you that you answer His call in your freedom. Therefore, little children, set time during the day when you can pray in peace and humility and meet with God the creator. I am with you and intercede with God for you. So, be on watch that every encounter in prayer may be a joyful meeting with God. Thank you for having responded to my call.

December 25, 1988: Dear children, I call you to peace. Live it in your heart and all around you, so that all will know peace, peace which does not come from you but from God. Little children, today is a great day. Rejoice with me; glorify the Nativity of Jesus through the peace that I give you. It is for this peace that I have come as your Mother, Queen of Peace. Today I give you my special blessing. Bring it to all creation, so that all of creation will know peace. Thank you for having responded to my call.

January 25, 1989: Dear children, today I am calling you to the way of holiness. Pray that you may comprehend the beauty and the greatness of this way where God reveals himself to you in a special way. Pray that you may be open to everything that God does through you that in your life you may be enabled to give thanks to God and to rejoice over everything that He does through each individual. I give you my blessing. Thank you for having responded to my call.

February 25, 1989: Dear children, today I invite you to prayer of the heart. Throughout this season of grace I wish each of you to be united with Jesus, but without unceasing prayer you cannot experience the beauty and greatness of the grace which God is offering you. Therefore, little children, at all times fill your heart with even the smallest prayers. I am with you and unceasingly keep watch over every heart which is given to me. Thank you for having responded to my call.

March 25, 1989: Dear children, I am calling you to a complete surrender to God. I am calling you to great joy and peace which only God can give. I am with you and I intercede for you every day before God. I call you, little children, to listen to me and to live the messages which I am giving you. For years you have been invited to holiness, but you are still far away. I am blessing you. Thank you for having responded to my call.

April 25, 1989: Dear children, I am calling you to a complete surrender to God. Let everything that you possess be in the hands of God. Only in that way shall you have joy in your heart. Little children, rejoice in everything that you have and give thanks to God because everything is God's gift to you. That way in your life you should be able to give thanks for everything and discover God in everything, even in the smallest flower. Thank you for having responded to my call.

May 25, 1989: Dear children, I am calling you to openness to God. You see, little children, how nature is opening herself and is giving life and fruits. In the same way I am calling you to a life with God and a complete surrender to Him. Little children, I am with you and unceasingly I desire to lead you into the joy of life. I desire that each one of you discovers the joy and the love which is found only in God and which only God can give. God wants nothing else from you but your surrender. Therefore, little children, decide seriously for

God because everything passes away. God alone does not pass away. Pray that you may discover the greatness and the joy of life which God is giving you. Thank you for having responded to my call.

June 25, 1989: Dear children, today I call you to live the messages which I have been giving you during the past eight years. This is a time of graces and I desire that the grace of God be great for every single one of you. I am blessing you and I love you with a special love. Thank you for having responded to my call.

July 25, 1989: Dear children, today I am calling you to renew your heart. Open yourself to God and surrender to Him all your difficulties and crosses so God may turn everything into joy. Little children, you cannot open yourselves to God if you do not pray; therefore, from today decide to consecrate a time and a day only for an encounter with God in silence. In that way you will be able, with God, to witness my presence here. Little children, I do not wish to force you; rather, freely give God your time, like children of God. Thank you for having responded to my call.

August 25, 1989: Dear children, today I call you to prayer. By means of prayer, little children, you will obtain joy and peace. Through prayer you are richer in the mercy of God. Therefore, little children, let prayer be the light for each one of you. Especially, I call you to pray so that all those who are far from God may be converted. Then our hearts shall be richer because God will rule in the hearts of all men. Therefore, little children, pray, pray, pray. Let prayer begin to rule in the whole world. Thank you for having responded to my call.

September 25, 1989: Dear children, today I invite you to give thanks to God for all the gifts you have discovered in the course of your life and even for the least gift you have received. I give thanks with you and want all of you to experience the joy of these gifts, and I want God to be everything for each one of you. And then, little children, you can grow continuously on the way of holiness. Thank you for having responded to my call.

October 25, 1989: Dear children, today also I am inviting you to prayer. I am always inviting you, but you are still far away. Therefore, from today, decide seriously to dedicate time to God. I am with you and I wish to teach you to pray with the heart. In prayer with the heart, you shall encounter God. Therefore, dear children, pray, pray, pray. Thank you for having responded to my call.

November 25, 1989: Dear children, I have been inviting you for years by these messages which I am giving you. Little children, by means of the messages I wish to make a very beautiful mosaic in your heart so I may be able to present each one of you to God like the original image. Therefore, little children, I desire that your decisions be free before God, because He has given you freedom. Therefore, pray so that, free from any influence of Satan, you may decide only for God. I am praying for you before God and I am seeking your surrender to God. Thank you for having responded to my call.

December 25, 1989: Dear children, today I bless you in a special way with my Motherly blessing and I intercede for you to God for Him to give you the gift of the conversion of the heart. For years I have been calling you to encourage you to a profound spiritual life in simplicity, but you are so cold! Therefore, little children, accept with seriousness and live the messages for your soul not to be sad when I will not be with you anymore and when I will not guide you anymore like an insecure child in his first steps. Therefore, little children, read every day the messages I gave you and transform them into life. I love you and this is why I call you to the way of salvation with God. Thank you for having responded to my call.

January 25, 1990: Dear children, today I invite you to decide for God once again and to choose Him before everything, so that He may work miracles in your life and that day by day your life may become joy with Him. Therefore, little children, pray and do not permit Satan to work in your life through misunderstandings, not understanding and not accepting one another. Pray that you may be able to comprehend the greatness and the beauty of the gift of life. Thank you for having responded to my call.

February 25, 1990: Dear children, I invite you to surrender to God. In this season (Lent), I want you to renounce all the things to which you are attached but that hurt your spiritual life. Therefore, little children, decide completely for God, and do not allow Satan to come into your life through those things that hurt both you and your spiritual life. Little children, God is offering Himself to you in fullness and you can discover and recognize Him only in prayer. Make a decision for prayer. Thank you for having responded to my call.

March 25, 1990: Dear children, I am with you, even if you are not conscious of it. I want to protect you from everything that Satan offers you, and through which, he wants to destroy you. As I bore Jesus in my womb, so also, dear children, do I want to bear you on to holiness. God wants to save you and send you messages through men, nature and so many things which can only help you to understand; but you must change the direction in your life. Therefore, little children, understand also the greatness of the gift which God is giving you through me, so that I may protect you with my Mantle and lead you to the joy of life. Thank you for having responded to my call.

April 25, 1990: Dear children, today I invite you to accept with seriousness and to live the messages which I am giving you. I am with you and I desire, dear children, that each of you be ever closer to my heart. Therefore, little children, pray and seek the will of God in your everyday life. I desire that each one of you discover the way of holiness and grow in it until eternity. I will pray for you and intercede for you before God that you receive the greatness of this gift which God is giving me that I can be with you. Thank you for having responded to my call.

May 25, 1990: Dear children, I invite you to decide with seriousness to live this Novena (for Pentecost). Consecrate the time to prayer and to sacrifice. I am with you and I desire to help you grow in renunciation and mortification that you may be able to understand the beauty of the lives of people who go on giving themselves to me in a special way. Dear children, God blesses you day after day and desires a change of your life. Thank you for having responded to my call.

June 25, 1990: Dear children, today, I desire to thank you for all your sacrifices and for all your prayers. I am blessing you with my special Motherly blessing. I invite you all to decide for God so that, from day to day, you will discover His will in prayer. I desire, dear children, to call all of you to a full conversion so that joy will be in your hearts. I am happy that you are here today in such great numbers. Thank you for having responded to my call.

July 25, 1990: Dear children, today I invite you to peace. I have come here as the Queen of Peace and I desire to enrich you with my Motherly Peace. Dear children, I love you and I desire to bring all of you to the peace which only God gives and which enriches every heart. I invite you to become carriers and witnesses of my peace to this unpeaceful world. Let peace rule in the whole world, which is without peace and longs for peace.

I bless you with my Motherly Blessing. Thank you for having responded to my call.

August 25, 1990: Dear children, today I invite you to take with seriousness and put into practice the messages which I am giving you. You know, little children, that I am with you and I desire to lead you along the same path to Heaven, which is beautiful for those who discover it in prayer. Therefore, little children, do not forget that these messages I am giving you have to be put into your everyday life in order that you might be able to say, "There, I have taken the messages and tried to live them." Dear children, I am protecting you before the Heavenly Father by my own prayers. Thank you for having responded to my call.

September 25, 1990: Dear children, I invite you to pray with the heart in order that your prayer may be a conversation with God. I desire that each of you dedicate more time to God. Satan is strong and wants to destroy and deceive you in many ways. Therefore, dear children, pray every day that your life will be good for yourself and all those in need. I am with you and I am protecting you even though Satan wishes to destroy my plan and to hinder the desires which the Heavenly Father wants to realize here. Thank you for having responded to my call.

October 25, 1990: Dear children, today I call you to pray in a special way, that you offer up sacrifices and good deeds for peace in the world. Satan is strong and, with all his strength, tries to destroy the peace which comes from God. Therefore, dear children, pray in a special way with me for peace. I am with you and I desire to help you with my prayers and I desire to guide you on the path of peace. I bless you with my Motherly Blessing. Do not forget to live the messages of peace. Thank you for having responded to my call.

November 25, 1990: Dear children, today I invite you to do works of mercy with love and out of love for me and your brothers and sisters. Dear children, all that you do for others do with great joy and humility toward God. I am with you and, day after day, I offer your sacrifices and prayers to God for the salvation of the world. Thank you for having responded to my call.

December 25, 1990: Dear children, today I invite you, in a special way, to pray for peace. Dear children, without peace, you cannot experience the birth of the Child Jesus today or in your daily lives. Therefore, pray that the Lord of Peace may protect you with His Mantle and that He help you to comprehend the greatness and the importance of peace in your hearts. In this way, you shall be able to spread peace from your hearts throughout the whole world. I am with you and I intercede for you before God. Pray, because Satan wants to destroy my plan of peace. Be reconciled with one another and, by means of your lives, work that peace may reign in the whole world. Thank you for having responded to my call.

January 25, 1991: Dear children, today, like never before, I invite you to prayer. Your prayer should be a prayer for peace. Satan is strong and wishes not only to destroy human life, but also nature and the planet on which you live. Therefore, dear children, pray that you can protect yourselves, through prayer, with the blessing of God's peace. God sends me to you so that I can help you if you wish to accept the rosary. Even the rosary alone can work miracles in the world and in your lives. I bless you and I stay among you as long as it is God's will. Thank you for not betraying my presence here, and I thank you because your response is serving God and peace. Thank you for having responded to my call.

February 25, 1991: Dear children, today I invite you to decide for God because distance from God is the fruit of the lack of peace in your hearts. God alone is peace. Therefore, approach Him through your personal prayer and then live peace in your hearts. In this way, peace will flow like a river into the whole world. Do not speak about peace, but make peace. I am blessing each of you and each good decision of yours. Thank you for having responded to my call.

March 25, 1991: Dear children, again today I invite you to live the passion of Jesus in prayer and in union with Him. Decide to give more time to God who gave you these days of grace. Therefore, dear children, pray and renew in a special way the love for Jesus in your hearts. I am with you and I accompany you with my blessings and my prayers. Thank you for having responded to my call.

April 25, 1991: Dear children, today I invite you so that your prayer be prayer with the heart. Let each of you find time for prayer so that in your prayer you discover God. I do not desire you to talk about prayer, but to pray. Let every day be filled with prayer of gratitude to God for life and for all that you have. I do not desire your life to pass by in words, but that you glorify God with deeds. I am with you, I am grateful to God for every moment spent with you. Thank you for having responded to my call.

May 25, 1991: Dear children, today I invite all of you who have heard my peace to realize it with seriousness and with love in your life. There are many who think they are doing a lot by talking about the messages but do not live them. Dear children, I invite you to life and to change all the negative in you so that it all turns into the positive, and into life. Dear children, I am with you and I desire to help each of you to live and, by living, to witness to the good news. I am here dear children, to help you and to lead you to heaven. In heaven is the joy through which you can already live heaven now. Thank you for having responded to my call.

June 25, 1991: Dear children, today, on this great day which you have given me, I desire to bless all of you and to say, "These days while I am with you are days of grace." I desire to teach you and to help you walk on the path of holiness. There are many people who do not desire to understand my message and to accept with seriousness what I am saying. But you, I therefore call and ask that, by your life and your daily living, you witness my presence. If you pray, God will help you discover the true reason for my coming. Therefore, little children, pray and read the Sacred Scriptures so that, through my coming, you may discover the message in Sacred Scripture for you. Thank you for having responded to my call.

July 25, 1991: Dear children, today I invite you to pray for peace. At this time, peace is threatened in a special way and I am seeking from you to renew fasting and prayer in your families. Dear children, I desire you to grasp the seriousness of the situation and that much of what will happen depends on your prayers; and you are praying a little bit. Dear children, I am with you and I am inviting you to begin to pray and fast seriously, as in the first days of my coming. Thank you for having responded to my call.

August 25, 1991: Dear children, today, also I invite you to prayer, now as never before, when my plan has begun to be realized. Satan is strong and wants to sweep away plans of peace and joy and make you think that my Son is not strong in His decisions. Therefore, I call all of you, dear children, to pray and fast still more firmly. I invite you to renunciation for nine days, so that, with your help, everything that I wanted to realize through the secrets which began at Fatima may be fulfilled. I call you, dear children, to grasp the importance of my coming and the seriousness of the situation. I want to save all souls and present them to God. Therefore, let us pray that everything I have begun will be fully realized. Thank you for having responded to my call.

September 25, 1991: Dear children, today, in a special way, I invite you all to prayer and renunciation. For now, as never before, Satan wants to show the world his shameful face, by which he wants to seduce as many people as possible onto the way of death and sin. Therefore, dear children, help my Immaculate Heart to triumph in the sinful world. I beseech all of you to offer prayers and sacrifices for my intentions so I can present them to God for what is most necessary. Forget your desires, dear children, and pray for what God desires and not for what you desire. Thank you for having responded to my call.

October 25, 1991: Pray! Pray! Pray! *Marija, the visionary who receives the monthly messages for the world, says Our Lady did not give her usual "Thank you for having responded to my call."*

November 25, 1991: Dear children, this time, also, I am inviting you to prayer. Pray that you might be able to comprehend what God desires to tell you through my presence and through the messages I am giving you. I desire to draw you ever closer to Jesus and His wounded heart, that you might be able to comprehend the immeasurable love which gave itself for each one of you. Therefore, dear children, pray that from your heart would flow a fountain of love to every person, both to the one that hates you and to the one that despises you. That way, you will be able, through Jesus' love, to overcome all the misery in this world of sorrow, which is without hope for those who do not know Jesus. I am with you and I love you with the immeasurable love of Jesus. Thank you for all your sacrifices and prayers. Pray so that I might be able to help you still more. Your prayers are necessary to me. Thank you for having responded to my call.

December 25, 1991: Dear children, today, in a special way, I bring the little Jesus to you that He may bless you with His blessings of peace and love. Dear children, do not forget that this is a grace which many people neither understand nor accept. Therefore, you who have said that you are mine and seek my help, give all of yourself. First of all, give your love and example in your families. You say that Christmas is a family feast; therefore, dear children, put God in the first place in your families so that He may give you peace and may protect you not only from war, but also protect you from every Satanic attack during peace. When God is with you, you have everything; but when you do not want Him, then you are miserable and lost and you do not know on whose side you are. Therefore, dear children, decide for God and then you will get everything. Thank you for having responded to my call.

January 25, 1992: Dear children, today, I am inviting you to a renewal of prayer in your families so that way every family will become a joy to my son Jesus.

Therefore, dear children, pray and seek more time for Jesus and then you will be able to understand and accept everything, even the most difficult sicknesses and crosses. I am with you and I desire to take you into my heart and protect you, but you have not yet decided. Therefore, dear children, I am seeking for you to pray, so through prayer you would allow me to help you. Pray, my dear little children, so prayer becomes your daily bread. Thank you for having responded to my call.

February 25, 1992: Dear children, today I invite you to draw still closer to God through prayer. Only that way will I be able to help you and to protect you from every attack of Satan. I am with you and I intercede for you with God, that He protect you. But I need your prayers and your "Yes." You get lost easily in material and human things, and forget that God is your greatest friend. Therefore, my dear little children, draw close to God so He may protect you and guard you from every evil. Thank you for having responded to my call.

March 25, 1992: Dear children, today as never before I invite you to live my messages and to put them into practice in your life. I have come to you to help you and, therefore, I invite you to change your life because you have taken a path of misery, a path of ruin. When I told you: "convert, pray, fast, be reconciled," you took these messages superficially. You started to live them and then you stopped, because it was difficult for you. No, dear children, when something is good, you have to persevere in the good and not think: God does not see me, He is not listening, He is not helping. And so you have gone away from God and from me because of your miserable interest. I wanted to create of you an oasis of peace, love and goodness. God wanted you, with your love and with His help, to do miracles and, thus, give an example. Therefore, here is what I say to you: Satan is playing with you and with your souls and I cannot help you because you are far away from my heart. Therefore, pray, live my messages and then you will see the miracles of God's love in your everyday life. Thank you for having responded to my call.

April 25, 1992: Dear children, today also I invite you to prayer. Only by prayer and fasting can war be stopped. Therefore, my dear little children, pray and by your life give witness that you are mine and that you belong to me, because Satan wishes in these turbulent days to seduce as many souls as possible. Therefore, I invite you to decide for God and He will protect you and show you what you should do and which path to take. I invite all those who have said yes to me to renew their consecration to my Son Jesus and to His Heart and to me so we can take you more intensely as instruments of peace in this unpeaceful world. Medjugorje is a sign to all of you and a call to pray and live the days of grace that God is giving you. Therefore, dear children, accept the call to prayer with seriousness. I am with you and your suffering is also mine. Thank you for having responded to my call.

May 25, 1992: Dear children, today also I invite you to prayer, so that through prayer you come still nearer to God. I am with you and I desire to lead you on the path to salvation that Jesus gives you. From day to day, I am nearer to you although you are not aware of it and you do not want to admit that you are only linked to me in a small way with your few prayers. When trials and problems arise, you say, "O God! O Mother! Where are you?" As for me, I only wait for your "Yes" to present to Jesus for Him to fill you with His grace. That is why, once more, please accept my call and start to pray in a new way until prayer becomes joy to you. Then you will discover that God is all-powerful in your daily life. I am with you and I am waiting for you. Thank you for having responded to my call.

June 25, 1992: Dear children, today I am happy, even if in my heart there is still a little sadness for all those who have started on this path and then have left it. My presence here is to take you on a new path, the path to salvation. This is why I call you, day after day to conversion. But if you do not pray, you cannot say that you are on the way to being converted. I pray for you and I intercede to God for peace; first peace in your hearts and also peace around you, so that God may be your peace. Thank you for having responded to my call.

July 25, 1992: Dear children, today also I invite you to prayer, a prayer of joy so that in these sad days no one amongst you may feel sadness in prayer, but a joyful meeting with God His Creator. Pray, little children, to be able to come closer to me and to feel through prayer what it is I desire from you. I am with you and each day I bless you with my maternal blessing so that Our Lord may fill you abundantly with His grace for your daily life. Give thanks to God for the grace of my being able to be with you because I assure you it is a great grace. Thank you for having responded to my call.

August 25, 1992: Dear children, today I desire to tell you that I love you. I love you with my maternal love and I invite you to open yourselves completely to me so that, through each one of you, I can convert and save this world which is full of sin and bad things. That is why, my dear little children, you should open yourselves completely to me so that I may carry you always further toward the marvelous love of God the Creator who reveals Himself to you from day to day. I am with you and I wish to reveal to you and show you the God who loves you. Thank you for having responded to my call.

September 25, 1992: Dear children, today again I would like to say to you that I am with you also in these troubled days during which Satan wishes to destroy all that my Son Jesus and I are building. He desires especially to destroy your souls. He wants to take you away as far as possible from the Christian life and from the commandments that the Church calls you to live. Satan wishes to destroy everything that is holy in you and around you. This is why, little children, pray, pray, pray to be able to grasp all that God is giving you through my coming. Thank you for having responded to my call.

October 25, 1992: Dear children, I invite you to prayer now when Satan is strong and wishes to make as many souls as possible his own. Pray, dear children, and have more trust in me because I am here in order to help you and to guide you on a new path toward a new life. Therefore, dear little children, listen and live what I tell you because it is important for you when I shall not be with you any longer that you remember my words and all that I told you. I call you to begin to change your life from the beginning and that you decide for conversion not with words but with your life. Thank you for having responded to my call.

November 25, 1992: Dear children, today, more than ever, I am calling you to pray. May your life become a continuous prayer. Without love you cannot pray. That is why I am calling you to love God, the Creator of your lives, above everything else. Then you will come to know God and will love Him in everything as He loves you. Dear children, it is a grace that I am with you. That is why you should accept and live my messages for your own good. I love you and that is why I am with you, in order to teach you and to lead you to a new life of conversion and renunciation. Only in this way will you discover God and all that which now seems so far away from you. Therefore, my dear children, pray. Thank you for having responded to my call.

December 25, 1992: Dear children, I desire to place all of you under my mantle and protect you from all satanic attacks. Today is a day of peace, but in the whole world there is a great lack of peace. That is why I call you all to build a new world of peace with me through prayer. This I cannot do without you, and this is why I call all of you with my motherly love and God will do the rest. So, open yourselves to God's plan and to His designs to be able to cooperate with Him for peace and for everything that is good. Do not forget that your life does not belong to you, but is a gift with which you must bring joy to others and lead them to eternal life. May the tenderness of the little Jesus always accompany you. Thank you for having responded to my call.

January 25, 1993: Dear children, today I call you to accept and live my messages with seriousness. These days are the days when you need to decide for God, for peace and for the good. May every hatred and jealousy disappear from your life and your thoughts, and may there only dwell love for God and for your neighbor. Thus, and only thus shall you be able to discern the signs of the time. I am with you and I guide you into a new time, a time which God gives you as grace so that you may get to know him more. Thank you for having responded to my call.

February 25, 1993: Dear children, today I bless you with my motherly blessing and I invite you all to conversion. I wish that each of you decide for a change of life and that each of you works more in the Church not through words and thoughts but through example, so that your life may be a joyful testimony for Jesus. You cannot say that you are converted, because your life must become a daily conversion. In order to understand what you have to do, little children, pray and God will give you what you completely have to do, and where you have to change. I am with you and place you all under my mantle. Thank you for having responded to my call.

March 25, 1993: Dear children, today like never I call you to pray for peace, for peace in your hearts, peace in your families and peace in the whole world, because Satan wants war, wants lack of peace, wants to destroy all which is good. Therefore, dear children, pray, pray, pray. Thank you for having responded to my call.

April 25, 1993: Dear children, today I invite you all to awaken your hearts to love. Go into nature and look how nature is awakening and it will be a help to you to open your hearts to the love of God, the Creator. I desire you to awaken love in your families so that where there is unrest and hatred, love will reign and when there is love in your hearts then there is also prayer. And, dear children, do not forget that I am with you and I am helping you with my prayer that God may give you the strength to love. I bless and love you with my motherly love. Thank you for having responded to my call.

May 25, 1993: Dear children, today I invite you to open yourselves to God by means of prayer so the Holy Spirit may begin to work miracles in you and through you. I am with you and I intercede before God for each one of you because, dear children, each one of you is important in my plan of salvation. I invite you to be carriers of good and peace. God can give you peace only if you convert and pray. Therefore, my dear little children, pray, pray, pray and do that which the Holy Spirit inspires you to do. Thank you for having responded to my call.

June 25, 1993: Dear children, today I also rejoice at your presence here. I bless you with my motherly blessing and intercede for each one of you before God. I call you anew to live my messages and to put them into life and practice. I am with you and bless all of you day by day. Dear children, these are special times and, therefore, I am with you to love and protect you; to protect your hearts from Satan and to bring you all closer to the heart of my Son, Jesus. Thank you for having responded to my call.

July 25, 1993: Dear children, I thank you for your prayers and for the love you show toward me. I invite you to decide to pray for my intentions. Dear children, offer novenas, making sacrifices wherein you feel the most bound. I want your life to be bound to me. I am your Mother, little children, and I do not want Satan to deceive you for He wants to lead you the wrong way, but he cannot if you do not permit him. Therefore, little children, renew prayer in your hearts, and then you will understand my call and my desire to help you. Thank you for having responded to my call.

August 25, 1993: Dear children, I want you to understand that I am your Mother, that I want to help you and call you to prayer. Only by prayer can you understand and accept my messages and practice them in your life. Read Sacred Scripture, live it, and pray to understand the signs of the times. This is a special time, therefore, I am with you to draw you close to my heart and the heart of my Son, Jesus. Dear little children, I want you to be children of the light and not of the darkness. Therefore, live what I am telling you. Thank you for having responded to my call.

September 25, 1993: Dear children, I am your Mother and I invite you to come closer to God through prayer because only He is your peace, your savior. Therefore, little children, do not seek comfort in material things, but rather seek God. I am praying for you and I intercede before God for each individual. I am looking for your prayers that you accept me and accept my messages as in the first days of the apparitions and only then when you open your hearts and pray will miracles happen. Thank you for having responded to my call.

October 25, 1993: Dear children, these years I have been calling you to pray, to live what I am telling you, but you are living my messages a little. You talk, but do not live, that is why little children, this war is lasting so long. I invite you to open yourselves to God and in your hearts to live with God, living the good and giving witness to my messages. I love you and wish to protect you from every evil, but you do not desire it. Dear children, I cannot help you if you do not live God's commandments, if you do not live the Mass, if you do not give up sin. I invite you to be apostles of love and goodness. In this world of unrest give witness to God and God's love, and God will bless you and give you what you seek from Him. Thank you for having responded to my call.

November 25, 1993: Dear children, I invite you in this time like never before to prepare for the coming of Jesus. Let little Jesus reign in your hearts and only then when Jesus is your friend will you be happy. It will not be difficult for you either to pray or offer sacrifices or to witness Jesus' greatness in your life because He will give you strength and joy in this time. I am close to you by my intercession and prayer and I love and bless all of you. Thank you for having responded to my call.

December 25, 1993: Dear children, today I rejoice with the little Jesus and I desire that Jesus' joy may enter into every heart. Little children, with the message I give you a blessing with my son Jesus, so that in every heart peace may reign. I love you, little children, and I invite all of you to come closer to me by means of prayer. You talk and talk but do not pray. Therefore, little children, decide for prayer. Only in this way will you be happy and God will give you what you seek from Him. Thank you for having responded to my call.

January 25,1994: Dear children, you are all my children. I love you. But, little children, you must not forget that without prayer you cannot be close to me. In these times Satan wants to create disorder in your hearts and in your families. Little children, do not give in. You should not allow him to lead you and your life. I love you and intercede before God for you. Little children, pray. Thank you for having responded to my call.

February 25, 1994: Dear children, today I thank you for your prayers. All of you have helped me so that this war may end as soon as possible. I am close to you and I pray for each one of you and I beg you: pray, pray, pray. Only through prayer can we defeat evil and protect all that Satan wants to destroy in your lives. I am your Mother and I love you all equally, and I intercede for you before God. Thank you for having responded to my call.

March 25, 1994: Dear children, today I rejoice with you and I invite you to open yourselves to me, and become an instrument in my hands for the salvation of the world. I desire, little children, that all of you who have felt the odor of holiness through these messages which I am giving you to carry, to carry it into this world, hungry for God and God's love. I thank you all for having responded in such a number and I bless you all with my motherly blessing. Thank you for having responded to my call.

April 25, 1994: Dear children, today I invite you to decide to pray according to my intention. Little children, I invite each one of you to help my plan to be realized through this parish. Now I invite you in a special way, little children, to decide to go along the way of holiness. Only this way will you be close to me. I love you and I desire to conduct you all with me to Paradise. But, if you do not pray and if you are not humble and obedient to the messages which I am giving you, I cannot help you. Thank you for having responded to my call.

May 25, 1994: Dear children, I invite you all to have more trust in me and to live my messages more deeply. I am with you and I intercede before God for you but also I wait for your hearts to open up to my messages. Rejoice because God loves you and gives you the possibility to convert every day and to believe more in God the Creator. Thank you having responded to my call.

June 25, 1994: Dear children, today I rejoice in my heart in seeing you all present here. I bless you and I call you all to decide to live my messages which I give you here. I desire, little children, to guide you all to Jesus because He is your salvation. Therefore, little children, the more you pray the more you will be mine and of my Son, Jesus. I bless you all with my motherly blessing and I thank you for having responded to my call.

July 25, 1994: Dear children, today I invite you to decide to give time patiently for prayer. Little children, you cannot say you are mine and that you have experienced conversion through my messages if you are not ready to give time to God every day. I am close to you and I bless you all. Little children, do not forget that if you do not pray you are not close to me, nor are you close to the Holy Spirit who leads you along the path to holiness. Thank you for having responded to my call.

August 25, 1994: Dear children, today I am united with you in prayer in a special way, praying for the gift of the presence of my most beloved son in your home country. Pray, little children, for the health of my most beloved son, who suffers, and whom I have chosen for these times. I pray and intercede before my Son, Jesus, so that the dream that your fathers had may be fulfilled. Pray, little children, in a special way, because Satan is strong and wants to destroy hope in your heart. I bless you. Thank you for having responded to my call.

September 25, 1994: Dear children, I rejoice with you and I invite you to prayer. Little children, pray for my intention. Your prayers are necessary to me, through which I desire to bring you closer to God. He is your salvation. God sends me to help you and to guide you towards paradise, which is your goal. Therefore, little children, pray, pray, pray. Thank you for having responded to my call.

October 25, 1994: Dear children, I am with you and I rejoice today because the Most High has granted me to be with you and to teach you and to guide you on the path of perfection. Little children, I wish you to be a beautiful bouquet of flowers which I wish to present to God for the day of All Saints. I invite you to open yourselves and to live, taking the saints as an example. Mother Church has chosen them, that they may be an impulse for your daily life. Thank you for having responded to my call!

November 25, 1994: Dear children, today I call you to prayer. I am with you and I love you all. I am your Mother and I wish that your hearts be similar to my heart. Little children, without prayer you cannot live and say that you are mine. Prayer is joy. Prayer is what the human heart desires. Therefore, get closer, little children, to my Immaculate Heart and you will discover God. Thank you for having responded to my call.

December 25, 1994: Dear children, today I rejoice with you and I am praying with you for peace: peace in your hearts, peace in your families, peace in your desires, peace in the whole world. May the King of Peace bless you today and give you peace. I bless you and I carry each one of your in my heart. Thank you for having responded to my call.

January 25, 1995: Dear children, I invite you to open the door of your heart to Jesus as the flower opens itself to the sun. Jesus desires to fill your hearts with peace and joy. You cannot, little children, realize peace if you are not at peace with Jesus. Therefore, I invite you to confession so Jesus may be your truth and peace. So, little children, pray to have the strength to realize what I am telling you. I am with you and I love you. Thank you for having responded to my call.

February 25, 1995: Dear children, today I invite you to become missionaries of my messages, which I am giving here through this place that is dear to me. God has allowed me to stay this long with you and therefore, little children, I invite you to live with love the messages I give and to transmit them to the whole world, so that a river of love flows to people who are full of hatred and without peace. I invite you, little children, to become peace where there is no peace and light where there is darkness, so that each heart accepts the light and the way of salvation. Thank you for having responded to my call.

March 25, 1995: Dear children, today I invite you to live peace in your hearts and families. There is no peace, little children, where there is no prayer and there is no love, where there is no faith. Therefore, little children, I invite you all, to decide again today for conversion. I am close to you and I invite you all, little children, into my embrace to help you, but you do not want and in this way, Satan is tempting you, and in the smallest thing, your faith disappears. This is why little children, pray and through prayer, you will have blessing and peace. Thank you for having responded to my call.

April 25, 1995: Dear children, today I call you to love. Little children, without love you can neither live with God nor with brother. Therefore, I call all of you to open your hearts to the love of God that is so great and open to each one of you. God, out of love for man, has sent me among you to show you the path of salvation, the path of love. If you do not first love God, then you will neither be able to love neighbor nor the one you hate. Therefore, little children, pray and through prayer you will discover love. Thank you for having responded to my call.

May 25, 1995: Dear children, I invite you, little children, to help me through your prayers so that as many hearts as possible come close to my Immaculate Heart. Satan is strong and with all his forces wants to bring closer the most people possible to himself and to sin. That is why he is on the prowl to snatch more every moment. I beg you, little children, pray and help me to help you. I am your mother and I love you and that is why I wish to help you. Thank you for having responded to my call.

June 25, 1995: Dear children, today I am happy to see you in such great numbers, that you have responded and have come to live my messages. I invite you, little children, to be my joyful carriers of peace in this troubled world. Pray for peace so that as soon as possible a time of peace, which my heart waits impatiently for, may reign. I am near to you, little children, and intercede for every one of you before the Most High. I bless you with my motherly blessing. Thank you for having responded to my call.

July 25, 1995: Dear children, today I invite you to prayer because only in prayer can you understand my coming here. The Holy Spirit will enlighten you to understand that you must convert. Little children, I wish to make of you a most beautiful bouquet prepared for eternity but you do not accept the way of conversion, the way of salvation that I am offering you through these apparitions. Little children, pray, convert your hearts and come closer to me. May good overcome evil. I love you and bless you. Thank you for having responded to my call.

August 25, 1995: Dear children, today I invite you to prayer. Let prayer be life for you. A family cannot say that it is in peace if it does not pray. Therefore, let your morning begin with morning prayer, and the evening end with thanksgiving. Little children, I am with you, and I love you and I bless you and I wish for every one of you to be in my embrace. You cannot be in my embrace if you are not ready to pray every day. Thank you for having responded to my call.

September 25, 1995: Dear children, today I invite you to fall in love with the Most Holy Sacrament of the Altar. Adore Him, little children, in your Parishes and in this way you will be united with the entire world. Jesus will become your friend and you will not talk of Him like someone whom you barely know. Unity with Him will be a joy for you and you will become witnesses to the love of Jesus that He has for every creature. Little children, when you adore Jesus you are also close to me. Thank you for having responded to my call.

October 25, 1995: Dear children, today I invite you to go into nature because there you will meet God the Creator. Today I invite you, little children, to thank

God for all that He gives you. In thanking Him you will discover the Most High and all the goods that surround you. Little children, God is great and His love for every creature is great. Therefore, pray to be able to understand the love and goodness of God. In the goodness and the love of God the Creator, I also am with you as a gift. Thank you for having responded to my call.

November 25, 1995: Dear children, today I invite you that each of you begin again to love, in the first place, God who saved and redeemed each of you, and then brothers and sisters in your proximity. Without love, little children, you cannot grow in holiness and cannot do good deeds. Therefore, little children, pray without ceasing that God reveals His love to you. I have invited all of you to unite yourselves with me and to love. Today I am with you and invite you to discover love in your hearts and in the families. For God to live in your hearts, you must love. Thank you for having responded to my call.

December 25, 1995: Dear children, today I also rejoice with you and I bring you little Jesus, so that He may bless you. I invite you, dear children, so that your life may be united with Him. Jesus is the King of Peace and only He can give you the peace that you seek. I am with you and I present you to Jesus in a special way, now in this new time in which one should decide for Him. This time is the time of grace. Thank you for having responded to my call.

January 25, 1996: Dear children, today I invite you to decide for peace. Pray that God give you the true peace. Live peace in your hearts and you will understand, dear children, that peace is the gift of God. Dear children, without love you cannot live peace. The fruit of peace is love and the fruit of love is forgiveness. I am with you and I invite all of you, little children, that before all else forgive in the family and then you will be able to forgive others. Thank you for having responded to my call.

February 25, 1996: Dear children, today I invite you to conversion. This is the most important message that I have given you here. Little children, I wish that each of you become a carrier of my messages. I invite you, little children, to live the messages that I have given you over these years. This time is a time of grace. Especially now, when the Church also is inviting you to prayer and conversion. I also, little children, invite you to live my messages that I have given you during the time since I appear here. Thank you for having responded to my call.

March 25, 1996: Dear children, I invite you to decide again to love God above all else. In this time when due to the spirit of consumerism one forgets what it means to love and to cherish true values, I invite you again, little children, to put God in the first place in your life. Do not let Satan attract you through material things but, little children, decide for God who is freedom and love. Choose life and not death of the soul, little children, and in this time when you meditate upon the suffering and death of Jesus I invite you to decide for life which blossomed through the Resurrection, and that your life may be renewed today through conversion that shall lead you to eternal life. Thank you for having responded to my call.

April 25, 1996: Dear children, today I invite you again to put prayer in the first place in your families. Little children, when God is in the first place, then you will, in all that you do, seek the will of God. In this way your daily conversion will become easier. Little children, seek with humility that which is not in order in your hearts, and you shall understand what you have to do. Conversion will become a daily duty that you will do with joy. Little children, I am with you, I bless you all and I invite you to become my witnesses by prayer and personal conversion. Thank you for having responded to my call.

May 25, 1996: Dear children, today I wish to thank you for all your prayers and sacrifices that you, during this month which is consecrated to me, have offered to me. Little children, I also wish that you all become active during this time that is through me connected to heaven in a special way. Pray in order to understand that you all, through your life and your example, ought to collaborate in the work of salvation. Little children, I wish that all people convert and see me and my son, Jesus, in you. I will intercede for you and help you to become the light. In helping the other, your soul will also find salvation. Thank you for having responded to my call.

June 25, 1996: Dear children, today I thank you for all the sacrifices you have offered me these days. Little children, I invite you to open yourselves to me and to decide for conversion. Your hearts, little children, are still not completely open to me and therefore, I invite you again to open to prayer so that in prayer the Holy Spirit will help you, that your hearts become of flesh and not of stone. Little children, thank you for having responded to my call and for having decided to walk with me toward holiness.

July 25, 1996: Dear children, today I invite you to decide every day for God. Little children, you speak much about God, but you witness little with your life. Therefore, little children, decide for conversion, that your life may be true before God, so that in the truth of your life you witness the beauty God gave you. Little children, I invite you again to decide for prayer because through prayer, you will be able to live the conversion. Each one of you shall become in their simplicity, similar to a child which is open to the love of the Father. Thank you for having responded to my call.

August 25, 1996: Dear children, listen, because I wish to speak to you and to invite you to have more faith and trust in God, who loves you immeasurably. Little children, you do not know how to live in the grace of God, that is why I call you all anew, to carry the word of God in your heart and in thoughts. Little children, place the Sacred Scripture in a visible place in your family, and read and live it. Teach your children, because if you are not an example to them, children depart into godlessness. Reflect and pray and then God will be born in your heart and your heart will be joyous. Thank you for having for responded to my call.

September 25, 1996: Dear children, today I invite you to offer your crosses and suffering for my intentions. Little children, I am your mother and I wish to help you by seeking for you the grace from God. Little children, offer your sufferings as a gift to God so they become a most beautiful flower of joy. That is why, little children, pray that you may understand that suffering can become joy and the cross the way of joy. Thank you for having for responded to my call.

October 25, 1996: Dear children, today I invite you to open yourselves to God the Creator, so that He changes you. Little children, you are dear to me. I love you all and I call you to be closer to me and that your love towards my Immaculate Heart be more fervent. I wish to renew you and lead you with my Heart to the Heart of Jesus, which still today suffers for you and calls you to conversion and renewal. Through you, I wish to renew the world. Comprehend, little children, that you are today the salt of the earth and the light of the world. Little children, I invite you and I love you and in a special way implore: Convert! Thank you for having responded to my call.

November 25, 1996: Dear children, today, again, I invite you to pray, so that through prayer, fasting and small sacrifices you may prepare yourselves for the coming of Jesus. May this time, little children, be a time of grace for you. Use every moment and do good, for only in this way will you feel the birth of Jesus in your hearts. If with your life you give an example and become a sign of God's love, joy will prevail in the hearts of men. Thank you for having responded to my call.

December 25, 1996: Dear children, today I am with you in a special way, holding little Jesus in my lap and I invite you, little children, to open yourselves to His call. He calls you to joy. Little children, joyfully live the messages of the Gospel, which I am repeating in the time since I am with you. Little children, I am your Mother and I desire to reveal to you the God of love and the God of peace. I do not desire for your life to be in sadness but that it be realized in joy for eternity, according to the Gospel. Only in this way will your life have meaning. Thank you for having responded to my call.

January 25, 1997: Dear children, I invite you to reflect about your future. You are creating a new world without God, only with your own strength and that is why you are unsatisfied and without joy in the heart. This time is my time and that is why, little children, I invite you again to pray. When you find unity with God, you will feel hunger for the word of God and your heart, little children, will overflow with joy. You will witness God's love wherever you are. I bless you and I repeat to you that I am with you to help you. Thank you for having responded to my call.

February 25, 1997: Dear children, today I invite you in a special way to open yourselves to God the Creator and to become active. I invite you, little children, to see at this time who needs your spiritual or material help. By your example, little children, you will be the extended hands of God, which humanity is seeking. Only in this way will you understand, that you are called to witness and to become joyful carriers of God's word and of His love. Thank you for having responded to my call.

March 25, 1997: Dear children, today, in a special way, I invite you to take the cross in your hands and to meditate on the wounds of Jesus. Ask of Jesus to heal your wounds, which you, dear children, during your life sustained because of your sins or the sins of your parents. Only in this way, dear children, you will understand that the world is in need of healing of faith in God the Creator. By Jesus' passion and death on the cross, you will understand that only through prayer you, too, can become true apostles of faith; when, in simplicity and prayer, you live faith which is a gift. Thank you for having responded to my call.

April 25, 1997: Dear children, today I call you to have your life be connected with God the Creator, because only in this way will your life have meaning and you will comprehend that God is love. God sends me to you out of love, that I may help you to comprehend that without Him there is no future or joy and, above all, there is no eternal salvation. Little children, I call you to leave sin and to accept prayer at all times, that you may in prayer come to know the meaning of your life. God gives Himself to him who seeks Him. Thank you for having responded to my call.

May 25, 1997: Dear children, today I invite you to glorify God and for the Name of God to be holy in your hearts and in your life. Little children, when you are in the holiness of God, He is with you and gives you peace and joy which come only from God through prayer. That is why, little children, renew prayer in your families and your heart will glorify the holy Name of God and heaven will reign in your heart. I am close to you and I intercede for you before God. Thank you for having responded to my call.

June 25, 1997: Dear children, today I am with you in a special way and I bring you my motherly blessing of peace. I pray for you and I intercede for you before God, so that you may comprehend that each of you is a carrier of peace. You cannot have peace if your heart is not at peace with God. That is why, little children, pray, pray, pray, because prayer is the foundation of your peace. Open your heart and give time to God so that He will be your friend. When true friendship with God is realized, no storm can destroy it. Thank you for having responded to my call.

July 25, 1997: Dear children, today I invite you to respond to my call to prayer. I desire, dear children, that during this time you find a corner for personal prayer. I desire to lead you towards prayer with the heart. Only in this way will you comprehend that your life is empty without prayer. You will discover the meaning of your life when you discover God in prayer. That is why, little children, open the door of your heart and you will comprehend that prayer is joy without which you cannot live. Thank you for having responded to my call.

August 25, 1997: Dear children, God gives me this time as a gift to you, so that I may instruct and lead you on the path of salvation. Dear children, now you do not comprehend this grace, but soon a time will come when you will lament for these messages. That is why, little children, live all of the words which I have given you through this time of grace and renew prayer, until prayer becomes a joy for you. Especially, I call all those who have consecrated themselves to my Immaculate Heart to become an example to others. I call all priests and religious brothers and sisters to pray the rosary and to teach others to pray. The rosary, little children, is especially dear to me. Through the rosary open your heart to me and I am able to help you. Thank you for having responded to my call.

September 25, 1997: Dear children, today I call you to comprehend that without love you cannot comprehend that God needs to be in the first place in your life. That is why, little children, I call you all to love, not with a human but with God's love. In this way, your life will be more beautiful and without any self-interest. You will comprehend that God gives Himself to you in the simplest way out of love. Little children, so that you may comprehend my words which I give you out of love, pray, pray, pray and you will be able to accept others with love and to forgive all who have done evil to you. Respond with prayer; prayer is a fruit of love towards God the Creator. Thank you for having responded to my call.

October 25, 1997: Dear children, also today I am with you and I call all of you to renew yourselves by living my messages. Little children, may prayer be life for you and may you be an example to others. Little children, I desire for you to become carriers of peace and of God's joy to today's world without peace. That is why, little children, pray, pray, pray! I am with you and I bless you with my motherly peace. Thank you for having responded to my call.

November 25, 1997: Dear children, today I invite you to comprehend your Christian vocation. Little children, I led and am leading you through this time of grace, that you may become conscious of your Christian vocation. Holy martyrs died witnessing: "I am a Christian and love God over everything." Little children, today also I invite you to rejoice and be joyful Christians, responsible and conscious that God called you in a special way to be joyfully extended hands toward those who do not believe, and that through the example of your life, they may receive faith and love for God. Therefore, pray, pray, pray that your heart may open and be sensitive for the Word of God. Thank you for having responded to my call.

December 25, 1997: Dear children, also today I rejoice with you and I call you to the good. I desire that each of you reflect and carry peace in your heart and say: "I want to put God in the first place in my life." In this way, little children, each of you will become holy. Little children, tell everyone, I want the good for you and he will respond with the good and, little children, good will come to dwell in the heart of each man. Little children, tonight I bring to you the good of my Son who gave His life to save you. That is why, little children, rejoice and extend your hands to Jesus who is only good. Thank you for having responded to my call.

January 25, 1998: Dear children, today again I call all of you to prayer. Only with prayer, dear children, will your heart change, become better, and be more sensitive to the Word of God. Little children, do not permit satan to pull you apart and to do with you what he wants. I call you to be responsible and determined and to consecrate each day to God in prayer. May Holy Mass, little children, not be a habit for you, but life. By living Holy Mass each day, you will feel the need for holiness and you will grow in holiness. I am close to you and intercede before God for each of you, so that He may give you strength to change your heart. Thank you for having responded to my call.

February 25, 1998: Dear children, also today I am with you and I, again, call all of you to come closer to me through your prayers. In a special way, I call you to renunciation in this time of grace. Little children, meditate on and live, through your little sacrifices, the passion and death of Jesus for each of you. Only if you come closer to Jesus will you comprehend the immeasurable love He has for each of you. Through prayer and your renunciation you will become more open to the gift of faith and love towards the Church and the people who are around you. I love you and bless you. Thank you for having responded to my call.

March 25, 1998: Dear children, also today I call you to fasting and renunciation. Little children, renounce that which hinders you from being closer to Jesus. In a special way I call you: Pray, because only through prayer will you be able to overcome your will and discover the will of God even in the smallest things. By your daily life, little children, you will become an example and witness that you live for Jesus or against Him and His will. Little children, I desire that you become apostles of love. By loving, little children, it will be recognized that you are mine. Thank you for having responded to my call.

April 25, 1998: Dear children, today I call you, through prayer, to open yourselves to God as a flower opens itself to the rays of the morning sun. Little children, do not be afraid. I am with you and I intercede before God for each of you so that your heart receives the gift of conversion. Only in this way, little children, will you comprehend the importance of grace in these times and God will become nearer to you. Thank you for having responded to my call.

May 25, 1998: Dear children, today I call you, through prayer and sacrifice, to prepare yourselves for the coming of the Holy Spirit. Little children, this is a time of grace and so, again, I call you to decide for God the Creator. Allow Him to transform and change you. May your heart be prepared to listen to, and live, everything which the Holy Spirit has in His plan for each of you. Little children, allow the Holy Spirit to lead you on the way of truth and salvation towards eternal life. Thank you for having responded to my call.

June 25, 1998: Dear children, today I desire to thank you for living my messages. I bless you all with my motherly blessing and I bring you all before my Son Jesus. Thank you for having responded to my call.

July 25, 1998: Dear children, today, little children, I invite you, through prayer, to be with Jesus, so that through a personal experience of prayer you may be able to discover the beauty of God's creatures. You cannot speak or witness about prayer, if you do not pray. That is why, little children, in the silence of the heart, remain with Jesus, so that He may change and transform you with His love. This, little children, is a time of grace for you. Make good use of it for your personal conversion, because when you have God, you have everything. Thank you for having responded to my call.

August 25, 1998: Dear children, today I invite you to come still closer to me through prayer. Little children, I am your mother, I love you and I desire that each of you be saved and thus be with me in Heaven. That is why, little children, pray, pray, pray until your life becomes prayer. Thank you for having responded to my call.

September 25, 1998: Dear children, today, I call you to become my witnesses by living the faith of your fathers. Little children, you seek signs and messages and do not see that, with every morning sunrise, God calls you to convert and to return to the way of truth and salvation. You speak much, little children, but you work little on your conversion. That is why, convert and start to live my messages, not with your words but with your life. In this way, little children, you will have the strength to decide for the true conversion of the heart. Thank you for having responded to my call.

October 25, 1998: Dear children, today I call you to come closer to my Immaculate Heart. I call you to renew in your families the fervor of the first days when I called you to fasting, prayer and conversion. Little children, you accepted my messages with open hearts, although you did not know what prayer was. Today, I call you to open yourselves completely to me so that I may transform you and lead you to the heart of my son Jesus, so that He can fill you with His love. Only in this way, little children, will you find true peace — the peace that only God gives you. Thank you for having responded to my call.

November 25, 1998: Dear children, today I call you to prepare yourselves for the coming of Jesus. In a special way, prepare your hearts. May holy Confession be the first act of conversion for you and then, dear children, decide for holiness. May your conversion and decision for holiness begin today and not tomorrow. Little children, I call you all to the way of salvation and I desire to show you the way to Heaven. That is why, little children, be mine and decide with me for holiness. Little children, accept prayer with seriousness and pray, pray, pray. Thank you for having responded to my call.

December 25, 1998: Dear children, in this Christmas joy I desire to bless you with my blessing. In a special way, little children, I give you the blessing of little Jesus. May He fill you with His peace. Today, little children, you do not have peace and yet you yearn for it. That is why, with my Son Jesus, on this day I call you to pray, pray, pray, because without prayer you do not have joy or peace or a future. Yearn for peace and seek it, for God is true peace. Thank you for having responded to my call.

January 25, 1999: Dear children, I again invite you to prayer. You have no excuse to work more because nature still lies in deep sleep. Open yourselves in prayer. Renew prayer in your families. Put Holy Scripture in a visible place in your families, read it, reflect on it and learn how God loves His people. His love shows itself also in present times because He sends me to call you upon the path of salvation. Thank you for having responded to my call.

February 25, 1999: Dear children, also today I am with you in a special way contemplating and living the passion of Jesus in my heart. Little children, open your hearts and give me everything that is in them: joys, sorrows and each, even the smallest, pain, that I may offer them to Jesus; so that with His immeasurable love, He may burn and transform your sorrows into the joy of His resurrection. That is why, I now call you in a special way, little children, for your hearts to open to prayer, so that through prayer you may become friends of Jesus. Thank you for having responded to my call.

March 25, 1999: Dear children, I call you to prayer with the heart. In a special way, little children, I call you to pray for conversion of sinners, for those who pierce my heart and the heart of my Son Jesus with the sword of hatred and daily blasphemies. Let us pray, little children, for all those who do not desire to come to know the love of God, even though they are in the Church. Let us pray that they convert, so that the Church may resurrect in love. Only with love and prayer, little children, can you live this time which is given to you for conversion. Place God in the first place, then the risen Jesus will become your friend. Thank you for having responded to my call.

April 25, 1999: Dear children, also today I call you to prayer. Little children, be joyful carriers of peace and love in this peaceless world. By fasting and prayer, witness that you are mine and that you live my messages. Pray and seek! I am praying and interceding for you before God that you convert; that your life and behavior always be Christian. Thank you for having responded to my call.

May 25, 1999: Dear children, also today I call you to convert and to more firmly believe in God. Children, you seek peace and pray in different ways, but you have not yet given your hearts to God for Him to fill them with His love. So, I am with you to teach you and to bring you closer to the love of God. If you love God above all else, it will be easy for you to pray and to open your hearts to Him. Thank you for having responded to my call.

June 25, 1999: Dear children, today I thank you for living and witnessing my messages with your life. Little children, be strong and pray so that prayer may give you strength and joy. Only in this way will each of you be mine and I will lead you on the way of salvation. Little children, pray and with your life witness my presence here. May each day be a joyful witness for you of God's love. Thank you for having responded to my call.

January 25, 2000: Dear children, I call you, little children, to pray without ceasing. If you pray, you are closer to God and He will lead you on the way of peace and salvation. That is why I call you today to give peace to others. Only in God is there true peace. Open your hearts and become those who give a gift of peace and others will discover peace in you and through you and in this way you will witness God's peace and love which He gives you. Thank you for having responded to my call.

February 25, 2000: Dear children, wake up from the sleep of unbelief and sin, because this is a time of grace which God gives you. Use this time and seek the grace of healing of your heart from God, so that you may see God and man with the heart. Pray in a special way for those who have not come to know God's love, and witness with your life so that they also can come to know God and His immeasurable love. Thank you for having responded to my call.

March 25, 2000: Dear children, pray and make good use of this time, because this is a time of grace. I am with you and I intercede for each one of you before God, for your heart to open to God and to God's love. Little children, pray without ceasing, until prayer becomes a joy for you. Thank you for having responded to my call.

April 25, 2000: Dear children, also today I call you to conversion. You are concerned too much about material things and little about spiritual ones. Open your hearts and start again to work more on your personal conversion. Decide everyday to dedicate time to God and to prayer until prayer becomes a joyful meeting with God for you. Only in this way will your life have meaning and with joy you will contemplate eternal life. Thank you for having responded to my call.

May 25, 2000: Dear children, I rejoice with you and in this time of grace I call you to spiritual renewal. Pray, little children, that the Holy Spirit may come to dwell in you in fullness, so that you may be able to witness in joy to all those who are far from faith. Especially, little children, pray for the gifts of the Holy Spirit so that in the spirit of love, every day and in each situation, you may be closer to your fellow man; and that in wisdom and love you may overcome every difficulty. I am with you and I intercede for each of you before Jesus. Thank you for having responded to my call.

June 25, 2000: Dear children, today I call you to prayer. The one who prays is not afraid of the future. Little children do not forget, I am with you and I love you all. Thank you for having responded to my call.

July 25, 2000: Dear children, do not forget that you are here on earth on the way to eternity and that your home is in Heaven. That is why, little children, be open to God's love and leave egoism and sin. May your joy be only in discovering God in daily prayer. That is why, make good use of this time and pray, pray, pray; and God is near to you in prayer and through prayer. Thank you for having responded to my call.

August 25, 2000: Dear children, I desire to share my joy with you. In my Immaculate Heart I feel that there are many of those who have drawn closer to me and are, in a special way, carrying the victory of my Immaculate Heart in their hearts by praying and converting. I desire to thank you and to inspire you to work even more for God and His kingdom with love and the power of the Holy Spirit. I am with you and I bless you with my motherly blessing. Thank you for having responded to my call.

September 25, 2000: Dear children, today I call you to open yourselves to prayer. May prayer become joy for you. Renew prayer in your families and form prayer groups. In this way, you will experience joy in prayer and togetherness. All those who pray and are members of prayer groups are open to God's will in their hearts and joyfully witness God's love. I am with you, I carry all of you in my heart and I bless you with my motherly blessing. Thank you for having responded to my call.

October 25, 2000: Dear children, today I desire to open my motherly heart to you and to call you all to pray for my intentions. I desire to renew prayer with you and to call you to fast which I desire to offer to my Son Jesus for the coming of a new time — a time of spring. In this Jubilee year many hearts have opened to me and the Church is being renewed in the Spirit. I rejoice with you and I thank God for this gift; and you, little children, I call to pray, pray, pray — until prayer becomes a joy for you. Thank you for having responded to my call.

November 25, 2000: Dear children, today when Heaven is near to you in a special way, I call you to prayer so that through prayer you place God in the first place. Little children, today I am near you and I bless each of you with my motherly blessing so that you have the strength and love for all the people you meet in your earthly life and that you can give God's love. I rejoice with you and I desire to tell you that your brother Slavko has been born into Heaven and intercedes for you. Thank you for having responded to my call.

December 25, 2000: Dear children, today when God granted to me that I can be with you, with little Jesus in my arms, I rejoice with you and I give thanks to God for everything He has done in this Jubilee year. I thank God especially for all the vocations of those who said 'yes' to God completely. I bless you all with my blessing and the blessing of the newborn Jesus. I pray for all of you for joy to be born in your hearts so that in joy you too carry the joy I have today. In this Child I bring to you the Savior of your hearts and the One who calls you to the holiness of life. Thank you for having responded to my call.

January 25, 2001: Dear children, today I call you to renew prayer and fasting with even greater enthusiasm until prayer becomes a joy for you. Little children, the one who prays is not afraid of the future and the one who fasts is not afraid of evil. Once again, I repeat to you: only through prayer and fasting also wars can be stopped — wars of your unbelief and fear for the future. I am with you and am teaching you little children: your peace and hope are in God. That is why draw closer to God and put Him in the first place in your life. Thank you for having responded to my call.

February 25, 2001: Dear children, this is a time of grace. That is why pray, pray, pray until you comprehend God's love for each of you. Thank you for having responded to my call.

March 25, 2001: Dear children, also today I call you to open yourselves to prayer. Little children, you live in a time in which God gives great graces but you do not know how to make good use of them. You are concerned about everything else, but the least for the soul and spiritual life. Awaken from the tired sleep of your soul and say yes to God with all your strength. Decide for conversion and holiness. I am with you, little children, and I call you to perfection of your soul and of everything you do. Thank you for having responded to my call.

April 25, 2001: Dear children, also today, I call you to prayer. Little children, prayer works miracles. When you are tired and sick and you do not know the meaning of your life, take the Rosary and pray; pray until prayer becomes for you a joyful meeting with your Savior. I am with you, little children, and I intercede and pray for you. Thank you for having responded to my call.

May 25, 2001: Dear children, at this time of grace, I call you to prayer. Little children, you work much but without God's blessing. Bless and seek the wisdom of the Holy Spirit to lead you at this time so that you may comprehend and live in the grace of this time. Convert, little children, and kneel in the silence of your hearts. Put God in the center of your being so that, in that way, you can witness in joy the beauty that God continually gives in your life. Thank you for having responded to my call.

June 25, 2001: Dear children, I am with you and I bless you all with my motherly blessing. Especially today when God gives you abundant graces, pray and seek God through me. God gives you great graces, that is why, little children make good use of this time of grace and come closer to my heart so that I can lead you to my Son Jesus. Thank you for having responded to my call.

July 25, 2001: Dear children, in this time of grace, I call you to come even closer to God through your personal prayer. Make good use of the time of rest and give your soul and your eyes rest in God. Find peace in nature and you will discover God the Creator Whom you will be able to give thanks to for all creatures; then you will find joy in your heart. Thank you for having responded to my call.

August 25, 2001: Dear children, today I call all of you to decide for holiness. Little children, may holiness be for you always in the first place in your thoughts and in each situation, in work and in speech. In this way, you will also put it into practice; little by little, step by step, prayer and a decision for holiness will enter into your family. Be real with yourselves and do not bind yourselves to material things but to God. And do not forget, little children, that your life is as passing as a flower. Thank you for having responded to my call.

September 25, 2001: Dear children, also today I call you to prayer, especially today when Satan wants war and hatred. I call you anew, little children: pray and fast that God may give you peace. Witness peace to every heart and be carriers of peace in this world without peace. I am with you and intercede before God for each of you. And you do not be afraid because the one who prays is not afraid of evil and has no hatred in the heart. Thank you for having responded to my call.

October 25, 2001: Dear children, also today I call you to pray from your whole heart and to love each other. Little children, you are chosen to witness peace and joy. If there is no peace, pray and you will receive it. Through you and your prayer, little children, peace will begin to flow through the world. That is why, little children, pray, pray, pray, because prayer works miracles in human hearts and in the world. I am with you and I thank God for each of you who has accepted and lives prayer with seriousness. Thank you for having responded to my call.

November 25, 2001: Dear children, in this time of grace, I call you anew to prayer. Little children, pray and prepare your hearts for the coming of the King of Peace, that with His blessing He may give peace to the whole world. Peacelessness has begun to reign in hearts and hatred reigns in the world. That is why, you who live my messages be the light and extended hands to this faithless world that all may come to know the God of Love. Do not forget, little children, I am with you and bless you all. Thank you for having responded to my call.

December 25, 2001: Dear children, I call you today and encourage you to prayer for peace. Especially today I call you, carrying the newborn Jesus in my arms for you, to unite with Him through prayer and to become a sign to this peaceless world. Encourage each other, little children, to prayer and love. May your faith be an encouragement to others to believe and to love more. I bless you all and call you to be closer to my heart and to the heart of little Jesus. Thank you for having responded to my call.

January 25, 2002: Dear children, at this time while you are still looking back to the past year I call you, little children, to look deeply into your heart and to decide to be closer to God and to prayer. Little children, you are still attached to earthly things and little to spiritual life. May my call today also be an encouragement to you to decide for God and for daily conversion. You cannot be converted, little children, if you do not abandon sins and do not decide for love towards God and neighbor. Thank you for having responded to my call.

February 25, 2002: Dear children, in this time of grace, I call you to become friends of Jesus. Pray for peace in your hearts and work for your personal conversion. Little children, only in this way will you be able to become witnesses of peace and of the love of Jesus in the world. Open yourselves to prayer so that prayer becomes a need for you. Be converted, little children, and work so that as many souls as possible may come to know Jesus and His love. I am close to you and I bless you all. Thank you for having responded to my call.

March 25, 2002: Dear children, today I call you to unite with Jesus in prayer. Open your heart to Him and give Him everything that is in it: joys, sorrows and illnesses. May this be a time of grace for you. Pray, little children, and may every moment belong to Jesus. I am with you and I intercede for you. Thank you for having responded to my call.

April 25, 2002: Dear children, rejoice with me in this time of spring when all nature is awakening and your hearts long for change. Open yourselves, little children, and pray. Do not forget that I am with you and I desire to take you all to my Son that He may give you the gift of sincere love towards God and everything that is from Him. Open yourselves to prayer and seek a conversion of your hearts from God; everything else He sees and provides. Thank you for having responded to my call.

May 25, 2002: Dear children, today I call you to put prayer in the first place in your life. Pray and may prayer, little children, be a joy for you. I am with you and intercede for all of you, and you, little children, be joyful carriers of my messages. May your life with me be joy. Thank you for having responded to my call.

June 25, 2002: Dear children, today I pray for you and with you that the Holy Spirit may help you and increase your faith, so that you may accept even more the messages that I am giving you here in this holy place. Little children, comprehend that this is a time of grace for each of you; and with me, little children, you are secure. I desire to lead you all on the way of holiness. Live my messages and put into life every word that I am giving you. May they be precious to you because they come from heaven. Thank you for having responded to my call.

July 25, 2002: Dear children, today I rejoice with your patron saint and call you to be open to God's will, so that in you and through you, faith may grow in the people you meet in your everyday life. Little children, pray until prayer becomes joy for you. Ask your holy protectors to help you grow in love towards God. Thank you for having responded to my call.

August 25, 2002: Dear children, also today I am with you in prayer so that God gives you an even stronger faith. Little children, your faith is small and you are not even aware how much, despite this, you are not ready to seek the gift of faith from God. That is why I am with you, little children, to help you comprehend my messages and put them into life. Pray, pray, pray and only in faith and through prayer your soul will find peace and the world will find joy to be with God. Thank you for having responded to my call.

September 25, 2002: Dear children, also in this peaceless time, I call you to prayer. Little children, pray for peace so that in the world every person would feel love towards peace. Only when the soul finds peace in God, it feels content and love will begin to flow in the world. And in a special way, little children, you are called to live and witness peace — peace in your hearts and families — and, through you, peace will also begin to flow in the world. Thank you for having responded to my call.

October 25, 2002: Dear children, also today I call you to prayer. Little children, believe that by simple prayer miracles can be worked. Through your prayer you open your heart to God and He works miracles in your life. By looking at the fruits, your heart fills with joy and gratitude to God for everything He does in your life and, through you, also to others. Pray and believe little children, God gives you graces and you do not see them. Pray and you will see them. May your day be filled with prayer and thanksgiving for everything that God gives you. Thank you for having responded to my call.

November 25, 2002: Dear children, I call you also today to conversion. Open your heart to God, little children, through Holy Confession and prepare your soul so that little Jesus can be born anew in your heart. Permit Him to transform you and lead you on the way of peace and joy. Little children, decide for prayer. Especially now, in this time of grace, may your heart yearn for prayer. I am close to you and intercede before

God for all of you. Thank you for having responded to my call.

December 25, 2002: Dear children, this is a time of great graces, but also a time of great trials for all those who desire to follow the way of peace. Because of that, little children, again I call you to pray, pray, pray, not with words but with the heart. Live my messages and be converted. Be conscious of this gift that God has permitted me to be with you, especially today when in my arms I have little Jesus — the King of Peace. I desire to give you peace, and that you carry it in your hearts and give it to others until God's peace begins to rule the world. Thank you for having responded to my call.

January 25, 2003: Dear children, with this message I call you anew to pray for peace. Particularly now when peace is in crisis, you be those who pray and bear witness to peace. Little children, be peace in this peaceless world. Thank you for having responded to my call.

February 25, 2003: Dear children, also today I call you to pray and fast for peace. As I have already said and now repeat to you, little children, only with prayer and fasting can wars also be stopped. Peace is a precious gift from God. Seek, pray and you will receive it. Speak about peace and carry peace in your hearts. Nurture it like a flower which is in need of water, tenderness and light. Be those who carry peace to others. I am with you and intercede for all of you. Thank you for having responded to my call.

March 25, 2003: Dear children, also today I call you to pray for peace. Pray with the heart, little children, and do not lose hope because God loves His creatures. He desires to save you, one by one, through my coming here. I call you to the way of holiness. Pray, and in prayer you are open to God's will; in this way, in everything you do, you realize God's plan in you and through you. Thank you for having responded to my call.

April 25, 2003: Dear children, I call you also today to open yourselves to prayer. In the foregone time of Lent you have realized how small you are and how small your faith is. Little children, decide also today for God, that in you and through you He may change the hearts of people, and also your hearts. Be joyful carriers of the risen Jesus in this peaceless world, which yearns for God and for everything that is from God. I am with you, little children, and I love you with a special love. Thank you for having responded to my call.

May 25, 2003: Dear children, also today I call you to prayer. Renew your personal prayer, and in a special way pray to the Holy Spirit to help you pray with the heart. I intercede for all of you, little children, and call all of you to conversion. If you convert, all those around you will also be renewed and prayer will be a joy for them. Thank you for having responded to my call.

June 25, 2003: Dear children, also today, I call you with great joy to live my messages. I am with you and I thank you for putting into life what I am saying to you. I call you to renew my messages even more, with new enthusiasm and joy. May prayer be your daily practice. Thank you for having responded to my call.

July 25, 2003: Dear children, also today I call you to prayer. Little children, pray until prayer becomes a joy for you. Only in this way each of you will discover peace in the heart and your soul will be content. You will feel the need to witness to others the love that you feel in your heart and life. I am with you and intercede before God for all of you. Thank you for having responded to my call.

August 25, 2003: Dear children, also today I call you to give thanks to God in your heart for all the graces which He gives you, also through the signs and colors that are in nature. God wants to draw you closer to Himself and moves you to give Him glory and thanks. Therefore, little children, I call you anew to pray, pray, pray and do not forget that I am with you. I intercede before God for each of you until your joy in Him is complete. Thank you for having responded to my call.

September 25, 2003: Dear children, also today I call you to come closer to my heart. Only in this way, will you comprehend the gift of my presence here among you. I desire, little children, to lead you to the heart of my Son Jesus; but you resist and do not desire to open your hearts to prayer. Again, little children, I call you not to be deaf but to comprehend my call, which is salvation for you. Thank you for having responded to my call.

October 25, 2003: Dear children, I call you anew to consecrate yourselves to my heart and the heart of my Son Jesus. I desire, little children, to lead you all on the way of conversion and holiness. Only in this way, through you, we can lead all the more souls on the way of salvation. Do not delay, little children, but say with all your heart "I want to help Jesus and Mary that all the more brothers and sisters may come to know the way of holiness." In this way, you will feel the contentment of being friends of Jesus. Thank you for having responded to my call.

November 25, 2003: Dear children, I call you that this time be for you an even greater incentive to prayer. In this time, little children, pray that Jesus be born in all hearts, especially in those who do not know Him. Be love, joy and peace in this peaceless world. I am with you and intercede before God for each of you. Thank you for having responded to my call.

December 25, 2003: Dear children, also today, I bless you all with my Son Jesus in my arms and I carry Him, who is the King of Peace, to you, that He grant you His peace. I am with you and I love you all, little children. Thank you for having responded to my call.

January 25, 2004: Dear children, also today I call you to pray. Pray, little children, in a special way for all those who have not come to know God's love. Pray that their hearts may open and draw closer to my heart and the Heart of my Son Jesus, so that we can transform them into people of peace and love. Thank you for having responded to my call.

February 25, 2004: Dear children, also today, as never up to now, I call you to open your hearts to my messages. Little children, be those who draw souls to God and not those who distance them. I am with you and love you all with a special love. This is a time of penance and conversion. From the bottom of my heart, I call you to be mine with all your heart and then you will see that your God is great, because He will give you an abundance of blessings and peace. Thank you for having responded to my call.

March 25, 2004: Dear children, also today, I call you to open yourselves to prayer. Especially now, in this time of grace, open your hearts, little children, and express your love to the Crucified. Only in this way, will you discover peace, and prayer will begin to flow from your heart into the world. Be an example, little children, and an incentive for the good. I am close to you and I love you all. Thank you for having responded to my call.

April 25, 2004: Dear children, also today, I call you to live my messages even more strongly in humility and love so that the Holy Spirit may fill you with His grace and strength. Only in this way will you be witnesses of peace and forgiveness. Thank you for having responded to my call.

May 25, 2004: Dear children, also today, I urge you to consecrate yourselves to my Heart and to the Heart of my Son Jesus. Only in this way will you be mine more each day and you will inspire each other all the more to holiness. In this way joy will rule your hearts and you will be carriers of peace and love. Thank you for having responded to my call.

June 25, 2004: Dear children, also today, joy is in my heart. I desire to thank you for making my plan realizable. Each of you is important, therefore, little children, pray and rejoice with me for every heart that has converted and become an instrument of peace in the world. Prayer groups are powerful, and through them I can see, little children, that the Holy Spirit is at work in the world. Thank you for having responded to my call.

July 25, 2004: Dear children, I call you anew: be open to my messages. I desire, little children, to draw you all closer to my Son Jesus; therefore, you pray and fast. Especially I call you to pray for my intentions, so that I can present you to my Son Jesus; for Him to transform and open your hearts to love. When you will have love in the heart, peace will rule in you. Thank you for having responded to my call.

This concludes the individual messages of Our Lady that are available at this time. The content of these messages obviously comprise a profound source of moral and spiritual truths, which would make up a veritable Marian Gospel.

Notes

---

[1] The doctrine of the Mystical Body of Christ as it appears in the encyclical **Mystici Corporis** describes the mysterious way in which Christ, who suffered once and for all for the sins of humanity at Calvary, continues to suffer in some sense through His extension in the members of His body, the Church. St. Paul, in his letter to the Colossians, also discusses the mystery of man being able to "complete what is lacking in the sufferings of Christ" (Col. 1:24).

Appendix

Revealed Prayers at Medjugorje

Prayers of Consecration to the Immaculate Heart of Mary

On April 19, 1983, Jelena Vasilj asked Mary how to consecrate oneself to her Immaculate Heart. Jelena reported receiving the following prayer of consecration (obtained from St. James Parish, Medjugorje):

O my Mother,
Mother of goodness, of love and mercy,
I love you infinitely,
and I offer myself to you.
Through your goodness, your love
and your grace, save me.
I love you infinitely,
and I desire that you protect me.
From the bottom of my heart I pray to you.
Mother of goodness,
give me your goodness.
Give it so that I may gain heaven through it.
I pray to you, for your infinite love,
to give me the graces

so that I may love each man,
as you loved Jesus Christ.
I pray that you may give me the grace
to be "merciful toward you," [1]
I offer myself totally to you and I desire
that you watch over my every step.

You are full of grace,
and I want to never forget this.
And if I should ever lose my graces,
I pray that you will restore them back to me.
Amen.

Prayer of Consecration to the
Sacred Heart of Jesus

This prayer of consecration to the Sacred Heart of
Jesus was reportedly dictated by the Blessed Virgin Mary
to Jelena Vasilj on November 28, 1983. It is followed by
a second prayer of consecration to the Immaculate Heart
of Mary, received on the same day:

O Jesus, we know that you have been gentle
and that you have offered your Heart for us.
It is crowned with thorns and with our sins.
We know that you pray every day
so that we may not be lost.

Jesus, remember us when we fall into sin.
Through your most holy Heart
make all people love one another.

Dispel hatred between men,
show us your love.
We all love you,
and desire that you protect us
with Your Shepherd's Heart
from every sin.

Enter into every heart, Jesus!
Knock, knock at the door of our hearts.
Be patient and persevering.
We are still closed because
we have not understood your will.

Knock continually!

O good Jesus, make us
open our hearts to You,
at least in the moment when
we remember Your passion,
suffered for us.
Amen.

Prayer of Consecration to the
Immaculate Heart of Mary

November 28, 1983.

O, Immaculate Heart of Mary, full of goodness,
show your love towards us.
That the flames of your heart, O Mary
may descend upon all humanity.

We love you immensely.
Imprint on our hearts true love
so that we may have everlasting desire for you.

O Mary, gentle and humble of heart,
remember us when we are in sin.
You know that all men sin.

Grant to us, through your immaculate and
maternal heart, to be protected from every
spiritual sickness.

Make us always look
To the goodness of your motherly heart;
and convert us through the flame
of your heart.
Amen.

The Rosary of Jesus Christ

The Rosary of Jesus Christ is a seven-point meditation on the life of Jesus, intermingled with other prayers and songs. Although a form of this rosary had been previously used by the Croatian Franciscans, this specific adaption was reportedly revealed by Mary through Jelena Vasilj, to be used by the youth prayer group at Medjugorje.

Begin with the recitation of the Creed.

Meditation 1 — How was Jesus born? In a cave of shepherds far from home, in extreme poverty. He turned to the humble before everyone else. He gave Himself above all to Mary and Joseph. How can Jesus be born in me? With my full conversion to Him. He finds in me the same poverty of Bethlehem, but if I open myself to Him, He makes me rich in Him. How can we make Him be born in others? By praying, fasting, witnessing with our actions . . .
Pause for meditation: a) five Our Fathers, slowly and with concentration; b) to be said with Mary — O God, be my strength and protection; c) an appropriate song (or a prayer to Mary).
Meditation 2 — How Jesus loves the poor, the weak, the outcast, the weary, the sick, the sinner. How shall I love them? Whom shall I prefer? How can I help them? How can I make amends for

sinners? How can I help **others** to love, in the example of Jesus?

Pause for meditation: a) five Our Fathers, slowly and with concentration; b) to be said with Mary — O God, be my strength and protection; c) an appropriate song (or a prayer to Mary).

Meditation 3 — How Jesus has been totally opened to God, outstretched to do His will. How shall I open myself to God with full availability to His will, even when it costs, convinced that it is for my greatest good? How can I **help others to open themselves**, to understand the gift of God's will?

Pause for meditation: a) five Our Fathers, slowly and with concentration; b) to be said with Mary — O God, be my strength and protection; c) an appropriate song (or a prayer to Mary).

Meditation 4 — How Jesus infinitely trusted His Father, even in the difficult moments. How shall I abandon myself in faith, and remove every fear from my heart? How can I reassure others, to spread trust and security in God's providence?

Pause for meditation: a) five Our Fathers, slowly and with concentration; b) to be said with Mary — O God, be my strength and protection; c) an appropriate song (or a prayer to Mary).

Meditation 5 — How Jesus was willing not only to listen to God, but also to give Himself to death on the cross. How shall I **give myself** to God until the end of my life out of love? How can I help others to give themselves totally to God, above all when they are called to the consecrated life?

Pause for meditation: a) five Our Fathers, slowly and with concentration; b) to be said with Mary — O God, be my strength and protection; c) an appropriate song (or a prayer to Mary).

Meditation 6 — How Jesus has conquered death, and has given to the Apostles the experience of the resurrection. How shall **I myself** rise from evil, experience the resurrection, communicate it? How can I bring others to the joy of the resurrection, to the hope of heaven?

Pause for meditation: a) five Our Fathers, slowly and with concentration; b) to be said with Mary — O God, be my strength and protection; c) an appropriate song (or a prayer to Mary).

Meditation 7 — How Jesus has risen to heaven and sent the Holy Spirit to the Apostles. How shall I, too, rise spiritually, with the grace of the Holy Spirit, reviving the hope of heaven? How can I help **others** to progress spiritually, calling upon them the Holy Spirit?

Pause for meditation: a) five Our Fathers, slowly and with concentration; b) to be said with Mary — O God, be my strength and protection; c) an appropriate song (or a prayer to Mary).

Conclude by reciting seven **Glory Bes.**

Notes

[1] *The prayer was distributed with the following footnote attached to it in reference to the noted verse in the fourth stanza.* Some theologians and priests have immediately stumbled on this verse and said: "How can a girl forgive the Blessed Mother?" "What has she to forgive the Blessed Mother for?" Others have immediately realized the profundity of the prayer, and they have recognized in the verse a part of spiritual life which is hidden from many Christians — the "pardonability to God."

The seer explains the verse as follows: "The Blessed Mother told me several times: 'Excuse me, but I can't give it to you, because it's not according to God's will.' Therefore, the phrase, 'I pray that you may give me the grace to be merciful towards you' means: 'Give me the grace of loving your will which is different from mine.'"